Eng. Parks Dept. Birmingham

Public Parks and Pleasure Grounds

Their cost, areas, and maintenance - bye-laws and regulations

Eng. Parks Dept. Birmingham

Public Parks and Pleasure Grounds

Their cost, areas, and maintenance - bye-laws and regulations

ISBN/EAN: 9783337193898

Printed in Europe, USA, Canada, Australia, Japan

Cover: Foto ©Suzi / pixelio.de

More available books at **www.hansebooks.com**

City of Birmingham.

PUBLIC PARKS
AND
PLEASURE GROUNDS.

THEIR COST, AREAS, AND MAINTENANCE;
BYE-LAWS AND REGULATIONS.

FEBRUARY, 1892.

J. COX, SECRETARY,
Parks Department.

Baths and Parks Committee, 1892.

Mr. Alderman R. C. BARROW, J.P., *Chairman.*
   Mr. Alderman W. WHITE, J.P.
   ,, Councillor E. W. BOWKETT.
   ,,   ,,   J. JACOBS, J.P.
   ,,   ,,   S. JOHNSON.
   ,,   ,,   R. NIXON.
   ,,   ,,   W. SHAMMON, J.P.
         ,,   J. WHATELEY.

Clerk to the Baths and Parks Committee:
Mr. W. S. PRITCHETT.

Superintendent and Engineer Baths Department:
Mr. J. COX.

Secretary Parks Department:
Mr. J. COX.

Superintendent of Parks:
Mr. S. HEARN.

Members of the Baths Sub-Committee.

Mr. Councillor E. W. BOWKETT, *Chairman.*
Mr. Councillor J. JACOBS, J.P.
  ,,   S. JOHNSON.
  ,,   W. SHAMMON, J.P.

Members of the Parks Sub-Committee.

Mr. Alderman W. WHITE, *Chairman.*
Mr. Councillor E. W. BOWKETT.
  ,,   ,,   S. JOHNSON.
  ,,   ,,   R. NIXON.
  ,,   ,,   W. SHAMMON, J.P.
  ,,   ,,   J. WHATELEY.

City of Birmingham.

POPULATION OF THE CITY (INCLUDING NEW DISTRICTS)	478,116
NUMBER OF BURGESSES ,, ,, ,,	88,186
NUMBER OF ALDERMEN AND COUNCILLORS ...	72
NUMBER OF WARDS	18
AREA IN ACRES	12,365
RATEABLE VALUE OF THE CITY (BEFORE THE ANNEXATION)	£1,817,638
BOROUGH RATE AT 2/5 IN THE £ FOR 1890-1 PRODUCED	£219,631
IMPROVEMENT RATE AT 2/1 IN THE £ FOR 1890-1 PRODUCED	£146,479
NUMBER OF PARKS AND GARDENS	14
NUMBER OF BATHING ESTABLISHMENTS	4
NUMBER OF OPEN-AIR SWIMMING BATHS	2

CONTENTS.

	Page
Establishment of Parks ...	7
Birmingham Parks Act, 1854 ...	14
Abstract from Public Health Act, 1875	19
,, ,, Birmingham Corporation Consolidation Act, 1883	20
,, ,, ,, Closed Burial Grounds	22
Bye-Laws and Regulations re Parks and Gardens	30
Special Regulations re Cannon Hill Park ...	34
,, ,, ,, Rednal and Bilberry Hills	34
Bye-Laws re Closed Burial Grounds ...	36
Adderley Park ...	43
Calthorpe Park ...	45
Aston Park ...	49
Cannon Hill Park	57
Highgate Park ...	61
Summerfield Park	63
Victoria Park, Small Heath ...	69
Burbury Street Recreation Ground ...	75
Walmer Recreation Ground ...	77
Nechells Recreation Ground ...	83
Closed Burial Grounds ...	85
St. Mary's Gardens	86
Park Street Gardens	86
St. Martin's Churchyard	87
Rednal and Bilberry Hills	89
Street Enclosures	95
Trees in Streets ...	95
Balsall Heath Recreation Ground	97
Detailed Statement of Annual Income from Parks and Gardens	98
,, ,, ,, ,, Expenditure ,, ,,	99
Summary of Details re Parks and Gardens	100
,, ,, ,, ,, ,, continued	101
,, ,, ,, ,, ,, ,,	102

CITY OF BIRMINGHAM.

PUBLIC PARKS, GARDENS, AND RECREATION GROUNDS.

THE first effort to obtain a Public Park for Birmingham was made in 1844, by means of a Committee appointed to raise a subscription for the provision of Parks and Gardens. The money raised (about £6,000) was, however, in 1846, applied for the purchase of the site of Kent Street Baths, and given to the Corporation by the subscribers.

In 1850, an ineffectual endeavour was made by the Town Council to purchase Aston Park, which is referred to more fully in the details relating to that Park.

In 1852, a large scheme for a Park was proposed by Mr. Samuel Beale, chairman of the Midland Railway Company, who, in 1841, was Mayor of Birmingham. This gentleman suggested that the Corporation should take 250 acres of land in Sutton Park on a lease for 999 years, at a rent of 1s. per acre, and that they should expend £20,000 in the erection of a Crystal Palace on the site; and, if the proposal was carried out, Mr. Beale undertook, on the part of the Midland Railway Company, that a railway should be constructed to Sutton, with a station adjoining the Palace. A Committee of the Council, to whom this project was referred, reported in 1853 that it had to be abandoned, because the Corporation of Sutton would neither grant a lease for a longer term than 99 years, nor let the land at less than £1 per acre.

These various proposals having failed, Birmingham, up to 1856, still remained one of the numerous towns which possessed no place appropriated to public recreation. In that year, Adderley Park was assigned to the Corporation by Mr. Charles Bowyer Adderley, on terms which practically amounted to a gift; and in the year following, Calthorpe Park was dedicated to the public use by the late Lord Calthorpe; and, subsequently, other desirable sites were obtained, either by purchase, or by the munificence of Miss Ryland, Mr. W. Middlemore, and others.

In the year 1854, a special Act of Parliament was obtained by the Council, whereby they were empowered to purchase land, and lay out the same, and charge the cost thereof on the rates of the Borough. This Act was called "The Birmingham Parks Act." And, under The Public Health Act of 1875, additional powers were granted to Local Authorities generally to acquire lands for the purpose of public pleasure grounds, etc. These powers were increased by The Birmingham Corporation Consolidation Act of 1883. Copies and abstracts of the several Acts are appended hereto.

The management and control of the Parks having been assigned to the Baths Committee by the Town Council, the general supervision of the first three Parks, viz.: Adderley Aston, and Calthorpe, was placed under the care of the late Superintendent of the Baths Department (Mr. B. Purnell) until 1866, when Mr. Alfred Rodway was appointed Superintendent of Parks, and Curator of Aston Hall, at a salary of £85 per annum, with residence at Aston Hall. Mr. Rodway's salary was subsequently increased to £250 per annum. His death took place on the 5th day of June, 1885.

On the 11th day of June following, a special meeting of the Baths and Parks Committee was held, to consider the appointment of a successor to the late Mr. Rodway. The Committee were then led to consider the desirability of separating the two offices hitherto held by him, as the Committee had already been in communication with the Museum and School of Art Committee, with a view of transferring the control of Aston Hall, with the objects of art therein, to that Committee, an arrangement which was subsequently accepted by the Museum and School of Art Committee, and approved by the Council on the 7th day of July, as per Council minute No. 13,826. The Baths and Parks Committee thereupon appointed Mr. Samuel Hearn (who had been Park-keeper at Cannon Hill Park from the date of opening) Superintendent of Parks, at a salary of £156 per annum, with residence at Cannon Hill Park as before; and a son of the late Superintendent was appointed to do the secretarial work of the Parks Department, at a salary of £104 per annum, jointly with his appointment by the Museum and School of Art Committee, as Curator of Aston Hall, at an additional salary of £52 per annum, with residence thereat.

On the 2nd day of July, 1889, the Baths and Parks Committee reported to the City Council that, with a view to the more economical and efficient discharge of the duties in connection with the secretarial work of the Parks Department, they had (subject to the approval of the Council) appointed Mr. J. Cox, the Superintendent and Engineer of the Baths Department, to be also Secretary of the Parks Department, so that in future the clerical work of the two departments would be carried on at the Kent Street office, and an annual payment of £60 would be made by the Parks Committee to the Baths Department in respect thereto. At the same meeting of the Council, the Committee reported that in consequence of the multiplicity of transactions in the two departments, and the involved nature of the accounts, they had appointed Messrs. Baker, Gibson, and Co., Chartered Accountants, of Bennetts Hill, to make a preliminary audit of the books for the half-year ending June 30th, and to report their recommendations thereon.

Messrs. Baker and Gibson subsequently reported their approval of the arrangements the Committee had made for the keeping of the accounts in the two departments, and they were thereupon duly appointed Auditors to the Baths and Parks Committee, the audit to be made at the end of each half municipal year.

There are about 50 men employed in the whole of the Parks and Gardens of the City, each Park being under the care of one Head Gardener, who resides in the Lodge attached thereto. The Park-keeper and the principal assistants are provided with uniform, and their wages range from 22s. to 28s. per week.

Under The Birmingham Consolidation Act, 1883, the Corporation secured powers to set apart a portion of the Public Parks or Recreation Grounds for games, such as football, cricket, lawn tennis, &c., and to make charges in respect thereto, with the result that in all the principal Parks such games are permitted, and the following charges are made:

For Cricket matches	- -	2s.6d. per match.
,, Junior clubs	- - -	1s.6d. ,, ,,
,, Lawn tennis, and use of nets		8d. per hour.
,, Croquet, and use of appliances		6d. ,, ,,
,, Football -	- - -	1s.0d. ,, match.
,, Lawn bagatelle and use of balls		8d. ,, hour.
,, Bowls, including use of same		3d. ,, ,,

The total income from these games at all the Parks is about £150 per annum.

No swings, trapeze, or other gymnastic appliances are provided or allowed in the Parks, and no charges are made for practising cricket or football therein, excepting in the case of special matches between rival clubs, which generally take place on Saturday afternoons; and, for the protection of the large number of visitors to the Parks on Bank Holidays, no cricket or football is allowed on those days, and in all cases the wickets must be pitched not less than 50 yards from any carriage drive or public footpath leading thereto.

The several Parks and Gardens are open to the public from 6 o'clock in the morning until sunset between the 31st March and 30th September, and at other times between sunrise and sunset, except when otherwise specially provided.

During the summer months the Police Band is engaged to give selections of music in the several Parks and Gardens, each evening alternately throughout the week, from 6 to 8 p.m., or from 7 to 9 p.m., and a charge of £18 per annum is paid to the Watch Committee in respect to each of the six principal Parks, or a total of £108. Following is the fixture each week for the Band Performance, from May to September:

VICTORIA PARK, SMALL HEATH	MONDAY EVENINGS.
SUMMERFIELD PARK	TUESDAY ,,
CALTHORPE PARK	WEDNESDAY ,,
HIGHGATE PARK	THURSDAY ,,
BURBURY STREET RECREATION GROUND AND PARK STREET GARDENS EVERY ALTERNATE	FRIDAY ,,
CANNON HILL PARK	SATURDAY ,,

Amateur Bands are also permitted to play in the Parks, subject to the approval of the Baths and Parks Committee, and providing their services are gratuitous, and no collections made or programmes sold in connection therewith. The Baths and Parks Committee invite offers from professional or amateur Bands to give selections of music in any of the Parks, subject to the conditions mentioned; and amongst those who have already gratuitously given their services, either weekly or occasionally, may be mentioned—Mr. Rainbow's Orchestral Amateur Band, which plays in Summerfield Park on Saturday evenings from 7 to 9 p.m., Messrs. W. and T. Wright's Band and Messrs. W. and T. Avery's Works Band give occasional performances in Victoria Park.

The Committee occasionally receive generous gifts of plants, seeds, shrubs, etc., for use in the ornamental portion of the Parks and Gardens; and many thousands of plants, such as geraniums, calceolarias, etc., are distributed annually amongst the poor, or given to the school children living in the neighbourhood of the several Parks, at the close of the season in September or October.

Boating Pools and open-air Swimming Baths are provided in Cannon Hill and Victoria Parks. The management of the Swimming Bath in Victoria Park is under the control of the Baths Committee, and the Swimming Bath in Cannon Hill Park is let to the lessee of the Refreshment Room and Boating Pools thereat. A uniform charge of 6d. per hour per person is made for boating in each of the Parks named, and fishing is permitted in the Pools on application to the lessee by payment of 1s. per rod.

Skating is allowed on the large Boating Pools during the winter free of charge (subject to the control of the Park-keepers as to the safety of the ice), and the Parks are occasionally kept open until 10 p.m. for that purpose.

Refreshment rooms are provided in Aston, Cannon Hill, Victoria, and Calthorpe Parks, and these are let to responsible tenants, who are the only persons authorised to sell refreshments in the Parks, the scale of charges being fixed by the Committee.

No intoxicating drinks are allowed to be sold in the Parks, and hawkers and pedlars are prohibited from vending their wares therein.

There are now seven Public Parks and seven Public Recreation Grounds, including Rednal Hill, Walmer Recreation Ground, and Balsall Heath Recreation Ground, now in course of formation, under the care of the Committee. The total loans borrowed on the several Parks and Gardens up to March 31st, 1891, is £76,092, to which must be added £9,700 for the purchase of additional land at Summerfield Park, which has subsequently been sanctioned by the Council, and also £2,200, the approximate cost of laying-out, fencing-in, and the erection of buildings in connection therewith. £2,100 has also been sanctioned by the Local Government Board for enclosing, laying-out, and erecting buildings in connection with the Walmer Recreation Ground, thus making a total capital expenditure up to September 30th of £90,092. The average annual amount of loans repaid during the three years ending March 31st, 1891, is £1,152, and the average annual amount of interest paid on loans for the same period is about £2,150; there will, however, be an increase of about £500 per annum for interest and sinking fund on the subsequent loans referred to. The average annual working expenditure on all the Parks and Gardens for the three years ending March 31st, 1891, amounts to £4,930, to which must be added £3,302, the average amount of interest and sinking fund for the same period, making a total annual expenditure of £8,232, equal to one and one-tenth of a penny in the £ on the rateable value of the City.

There is an annual income of about £650 derived from the various rents, grazing, &c.

The following are the various Acts and powers obtained by the Corporation in respect to the Purchase of Lands for the formation, maintenance, and regulation of the Public Parks and Gardens, and Closed Burial Grounds, etc.

AN ACT FOR ESTABLISHING PARKS IN OR NEAR TO THE BOROUGH OF BIRMINGHAM.

[ROYAL ASSENT, *July 3rd*, 1854.]

Preamble.

WHEREAS it would be greatly for the benefit of the inhabitants of the borough of Birmingham that there should be provided for their use parks and gardens for the purposes of healthful and pleasurable resort:

And whereas the purposes aforesaid cannot be effected without the authority of Parliament:

MAY IT THEREFORE PLEASE YOUR MAJESTY,

That it may be enacted, and Be it Enacted by the Queen's Most Excellent Majesty, by and with the advice and consent of the Lords Spiritual and Temporal and of the Commons in this present Parliament assembled, and by the authority of the same, as follows (that is to say):

Power for council to accept grants and make purchases of lands.

1. The council of the said borough, for the purpose of providing for the inhabitants of Birmingham, parks and other places of healthful and pleasurable resort, shall have power to do the following things, or any of them: To accept any gifts, grants, or devises of lands; or to purchase for a sum of money in gross or in consideration of an annual rent-charge, payable

by the council, any lands situate in or near Birmingham; to contribute towards the establishment by any person or bodies of persons of any such parks or places as aforesaid ; and for the purpose aforesaid to improve, maintain, and otherwise deal with such lands in such manner as they may deem most conducive to the purposes of this Act: Provided always, That in the case of any grant or conveyance made by parties not entitled to the absolute freehold and inheritance of the lands granted or conveyed, there may be contained covenants on the part of the council of the borough not to erect, set up, or exhibit, or to permit to be erected, set up, or exhibited in the said parks or places any shows or exhibitions, or any publichouses or houses of public entertainment, or any other conditions which the person granting the same may consider necessary : Provided also, That the council shall not erect any buildings on the said lands except such as may be required for the purposes of this Act.

Incorporation of "Lands Clauses Act, 1845."

2. " The Lands Clauses Consolidation Act, 1845," except the sections with respect to the purchase of lands otherwise than by agreement, is hereby incorporated with this Act.

Power to levy money.

3. The council of the said borough may levy with and as part of the borough rate levied in the said borough, or by a separate rate to be levied in like manner as the said borough rate, and may take out of the borough fund such sums of money as they may from time to time deem needful for the purpose of carrying into effect any of the objects of this Act; Provided that the whole increase in the said borough rate for any one year, for the purposes of this Act, do not exceed one penny in the pound, or if a separate rate be levied, that such rate do not exceed one penny in the pound of the annual value of the property in the borough rateable to the borough rate.

Power to borrow money.

4. The council shall have power from time to time to borrow at interest for the purposes of this Act, on the security

of the increase hereby authorised to be made to the said borough rate, or of the separate rate authorized by this Act, any sum or sums of money not exceeding the sum of thirty thousand pounds, and the money so borrowed shall be repaid within thirty years from the time of borrowing the same; and the mortgagees under this Act may enforce the payment of any arrears of interest or the arrears of principal and interest due to them by the appointment of a receiver, and the amount owing to the mortgagees by whom application for such receiver shall be made, shall not be less than five thousand pounds; and for the purposes aforesaid the clauses of "The Commissioners' Clauses Act, 1847," with respect to the mortgages to be executed by the commissioners (except the clause numbered 84), shall be incorporated with this Act.

Lands to be vested in the Corporation.

5. All lands so accepted or purchased, or taken and acquired, as aforesaid, shall be vested in and held upon trust for ever, or for such estate and interest as shall be acquired therein, by the mayor, aldermen, and burgesses of the said borough of Birmingham, and shall be managed by the council of the borough, and kept in fit and proper order for the benefit of the inhabitants of the said borough of Birmingham and others resorting thereto.

Saving rights of Reversioner in Leaseholds.

6. Provided always, That if under the powers of this Act the council of the said borough shall become possessed of or entitled to any leasehold estate or interest in any lands, then and in every such case the council of the said borough, in respect of such lands, shall be and remain subject and liable to the rent and other payments, and to the performance and observance of all covenants, conditions, restrictions, and agreements reserved by and contained in the lease of such lands, as fully and effectually as the original lessee under such lease would have been if he had not disposed of the same; and nothing in this Act contained shall release or discharge such lands, or the council of the said borough, in respect thereof,

from such rent or payments, or from the performance or
observance of any such covenants, conditions, restrictions, or
agreements, unless and until they shall have purchased or
otherwise lawfully acquired the reversion in such lands, or the
discharge thereof, from such rent and payments, and from the
performance and observance of such covenants, conditions,
restrictions, and agreements.

*Power for Council to appropriate Land as a Site for
Public Libraries.*

7. The council shall have power to appropriate any
portion of the land vested in the said mayor, aldermen, and burgesses under this Act as a site for any buildings that may be
erected in pursuance of "The Public Libraries Act, 1850," and
to erect thereon such buildings accordingly.

*Lands not to be Alienated or Exchanged without the consent of
Lords Commissioners of Her Majesty's Treasury.*

8. It shall not be lawful for the council to alienate or
exchange the lands to be acquired by them under the provisions
of this Act without the consent of the Lords Commissioners
of Her Majesty's Treasury, and it shall be lawful for such
council, with the approbation of the said Lords Commissioners,
or any three of them, to alienate or exchange any of such
lands, in such manner and on such terms and conditions as
shall have been approved by such Lords Commissioners;
Provided always, That notice of the intention of the council to
make application to the Lords Commissioners for such approval
shall be fixed on the outer door of the Town Hall, or in some
public and conspicuous place within the borough, one calendar
month at least before such application, and a copy of the
memorial intended to be sent to the said Lords Commissioners
shall be kept in the Town Clerk's office during such calendar
month, and shall be freely open to the inspection of every
burgess at all reasonable hours during the same.

Power of Council to make Bye-laws.

9. The council of the said borough may make such byelaws and regulations as they may think expedient, for the

purpose of carrying into effect the objects of this Act, and may annex reasonable penalties for the breach of such bye-laws and regulations, or any of them ; Provided that no penalty so to be appointed shall exceed the sum of five pounds, and that no such bye-law shall be made unless at least two-thirds of the whole number of the council shall be present; Provided that no such bye-law shall be of any force until the expiration of forty days after the same, or a copy thereof, shall have been sent, sealed with the seal of the said borough, to one of Her Majesty's principal Secretaries of State, and shall have been affixed on the outer door of the Town Hall, or in some other public place, within such borough ; and if at any time within the said period of forty days, Her Majesty, with the advice of Her Privy Council, shall disallow the same bye-law, or any part thereof, such bye-law, or the part disallowed, shall not come into operation ; Provided also, That it shall be lawful for Her Majesty, if she shall think fit, at any time within the said period of forty days, to enlarge the time within which such bye-law, if disallowed, shall not come into force ; and no such bye-law shall in that case come into force until after the expiration of such enlarged time.

Expenses of Act.

10. All costs, charges, and expenses of and attending the passing of this Act, or incidental thereto, may be paid by the council of the said borough out of the borough fund.

Short Title of Act.

11. This Act may be cited for all purposes as "The Birmingham Parks Act, 1854"

ABSTRACT FROM PUBLIC HEALTH ACT, 1875 (38 AND 39 VICT., CH. 55), RELATING TO PUBLIC PLEASURE GROUNDS, ETC.

Section 164. Any urban authority may purchase or take on lease, lay out, plant, improve, and maintain lands for the purpose of being used as public walks or pleasure grounds, and may support or contribute to the support of public walks or pleasure grounds, provided by any person whomsoever.

Any urban authority may make bye-laws for the regulation of any such public walk or pleasure ground, and may, by such bye-laws, provide for the removal from such public walk or pleasure ground of any person infringing any such bye-law by any officer of the urban authority or constable.

Section 165. Any urban authority may from time to time provide such clocks as they consider necessary, and cause them to be fixed on or against any public building, or, with the consent of the owner or occupier, on or against any private building, the situation of which may be convenient for that purpose, and may cause the dials thereof to be lighted at night, and may from time to time alter and remove any such clocks to such other like situation as they may consider expedient.

FOLLOWING IS AN ABSTRACT OF THE VARIOUS POWERS OBTAINED BY THE CITY COUNCIL IN RESPECT TO THE PURCHASE OF LANDS FOR THE FORMATION, MAINTENANCE, AND REGULATION OF PUBLIC PARKS AND GARDENS, INCLUDING THE CLOSED BURIAL GROUNDS, AND THE BYE-LAWS UNDER THE BIRMINGHAM CORPORATION CONSOLIDATION ACT, 1883.

PARKS.

Power to purchase lands for formation of Parks and to form Parks.

Section 67. The Corporation may from time to time purchase by agreement, or accept a gift of, or contribute to the acquisition of any lands within or without the Borough, to be appropriated for the purposes of a park or a public walk or public walks, or a place or places of public resort or recreation, or of the enlargement or improvement thereof, or of the approaches thereto; and may level, drain, sewer, pave, flag, gravel, lay out, plant, light, or otherwise improve any such park, walk, or place, and do such other acts as appear necessary to the Corporation, with a view to the proper formation, maintenance, improvement, use, and enjoyment of every such park, walk, or place.

Maintenance and Improvement of Parks.

Section 68. The Corporation may from time to time maintain, re-arrange, improve, and ornament any park, public walk, or place of public resort or recreation belonging to them, and may erect on any part of the same refreshment rooms, shelters, and other like buildings and conveniences for the use of the public, and buildings and conveniences for storing and keeping tools and materials; and they may, for the purpose of improving and ornamenting such parks, walks, and other places, and the approaches thereto, execute and make such works, roads, and conveniences as they may from time to time think necessary or expedient.

Power to set apart ground for Games.

Section 69. The Corporation may set apart portions of the parks and recreation grounds for cricket, football, archery, and other like games ; or for the exercise, inspection, or review of any portion of Her Majesty's forces, but so that the same shall be open to the public when not in use for such games or for such purposes as aforesaid.

Bye-laws for Regulation of Parks, &c.

Section 70. The Corporation may from time to time make Bye-laws relating to any park, public walk, or place of public resort or recreation belonging to them, for all or any of the purposes following (that is to say) :

For regulating the conduct of persons frequenting the same.

For preventing the holding therein of any religious, political, or party meeting, or any meeting which, in the judgment of the Corporation, is not proper to be held therein.

For regulating refreshment rooms therein, and for determining the days on and hours at which they are to be opened and closed, and the nature and prices of the articles to be sold therein.

For preventing or for regulating the smoking of tobacco in any building, or part of a building therein.

For preventing or regulating the admission therein of dogs.

For preventing males from intruding on or using places therein set apart for the use of females, or *vice versâ*.

For preventing or regulating the admission therein of vehicles, horses, and other animals.

For protecting from injury buildings, terraces, fountains, bridges, walks, seats, fences, and other parts of, or things of or belonging to the park, walk, or place ; and for preventing the destruction or injury of aquatic or other birds, their nests or eggs, or of other animals, or of fish, or of trees, shrubs, plants, and flowers, or the plucking of flowers and leaves therein.

For enabling the servants of the Corporation to remove therefrom persons guilty of a breach of any bye-law relative thereto.

Power to regulate hours of opening and closing, and other matters.

Section 71. The Corporation may from time to time, as respects any park, public walk, or place of public resort or recreation belonging to them, make regulations for regulating the hours of opening and closing the same, the payment to be made for admission to any building therein, or for the use of any ground for cricket or any other game.

Park-keepers to be made Constables.

Section 72. The Corporation may cause any Park-keepers appointed by the Corporation, and all persons appointed to assist them, permanently or otherwise, to make such declaration as is by law required to be made by constables of the Borough; and the men making such declaration shall (if in uniform, or provided with a warrant, which they shall show if required) have, in the parks (whether within or beyond the borough) for the time being belonging to or under the control of the Corporation, such powers, authorities, and privileges, and shall be liable to such responsibilities, and (subject to the directions of the Corporation) shall perform all such duties as constables appointed under The Municipal Corporations Act, 1882.

POWERS RELATING TO CLOSED BURIAL GROUNDS.

Meaning of Closed Burial Ground.

Section 193. For the purposes of this Act, the expression " Closed Burial Ground " means any burial or part of a burial ground within the Borough which is for the time being wholly or partially closed for burials, under the provisions of any Statute or Order in Council.

Power to Incumbents, etc., to grant to Corporations rights over Closed Burial Grounds.

Section 199. Subject to the provisions and for any of the purposes of this Act, the persons hereinafter mentioned may, with the consent of the Secretary of State, grant to the Corporation, and the Corporation may accept from time to time, either the absolute property, or any less estate, right, or easement in or over the whole or any part of any Closed Burial Ground.

Persons by whom Grants may be made.

Section 200. A grant for the purpose of this Act may be made to the Corporation by the following persons (that is to say):

(1) In the case of a Closed Burial Ground belonging to any parish (whether the same is an ancient parish, or is a parish or district for ecclesiastical purposes) by the actual Incumbent of the benefice of such parish (whether such Incumbent be Rector, Vicar, or Perpetual Curate), with, in any case, the previous consent, in writing, of the Bishop of the diocese, which shall be recited in the grant, or testified by his signature thereto.

(2) In the case of a Closed Burial Ground belonging to two or more such parishes, by the actual Incumbents thereof, as hereinbefore defined, and with the like consent.

(3) In the case of a Closed Burial Ground which is vested in trustees or commissioners, by such trustees or commissioners, or the major part of them, respectively.

(4) In any other case, by the owners in fee of the Closed Burial Ground.

Provision where owners unknown.

Section 201. In the case of any Closed Burial Ground not belonging to any parish or parishes as aforesaid, and not vested in trustees, or the trustees of which cannot be found, or in the case of which no person capable of making a grant as aforesaid under this Act exists or is known, the Corporation, after giving notice by advertisements or otherwise, as they may be directed by the Secretary of State, may take possession of and use such burial ground for the purpose of this Act; and in case no person within ten years after such notice has been given establishes by action or otherwise a title to such burial ground, or a right to control the use of the same, the same shall, at the end of such ten years, vest in the Corporation absolutely for the purposes of this Act.

Consideration for Grants.

Section 202. A grant under this Act may be made with or without any valuable consideration. Any such consideration shall be made either by way of periodical payment, or by payment of a gross sum, and shall be secured and paid in such manner as the Corporation, with the approval of the Secretary of State, determines; but so that in the case of a Closed Burial Ground belonging to a parish or parishes, the benefit of any such payment shall be secured to the Incumbent or Incumbents for the time being by way of annual income, as nearly as may be, as if it had arisen from the sale of lands belonging to the benefice; or the consideration of a gross sum may, with the consent of the Incumbent, be applied for such purposes in connection with his church or parish as the Bishop of the diocese and the Secretary of State may approve.

Form of Grant.

Section 203. A grant for the purposes of this Act may be in the form contained in the Seventh Schedule of this Act, or to the like effect, and every grant so made shall be effectual for the purposes therein expressed; but every such grant shall bear the proper *ad valorem* or other stamp duty to which it may be liable under the Acts in force relating to Stamp Duties.

Powers of Corporation under Grants.

Section 204. When, under the provisions of this Act, the Corporation have become possessed of any Closed Burial Ground, or part of a Closed Burial Ground, or of any estate, rights, or easements in or over the same, it shall be lawful for them (subject to any conditions or restrictions contained in the grant, and so far only as the grant shall extend) from time to time to do all or any of the following things with respect to such Closed Burial Ground or part thereof (that is to say):

(1) To lay out, level, repair, turf, plant, embellish, light, improve, and maintain the same.

(2) To fence the same or any part thereof, or to throw open the same or any part thereof to the public.

(3) To lay out and maintain walks or footways through or over the same.

(4) To provide seats for the use of the public.

(5) Generally to maintain the same, and any graves, tombs, or monuments therein, in decent order and in a proper sanitary condition.

(6) Where it is expedient, for the purpose of widening or improving any street, to lay out, level, pave, fence, and maintain such part of the same as may be necessary as part of such street; but this power shall not be exercised without the consent of the Secretary of State.

(7) To regulate and control the use of the same by the public.

To the extent to which the Corporation are under any such grant entitled to maintain and keep in order any Closed Burial Ground, and any graves, tombs, or monuments therein, it shall be their duty so to do; and no other person, body, or corporation shall to that extent be under any liability in respect thereof.

Preservation of Freehold of Site of Church in Incumbent.

Section 205. When a church stands in a Closed Burial Ground, the freehold of the site of the church, with all right of way to and from the same, shall be preserved to the Incumbent or persons entitled to use the same; and in case it shall be expedient to re-build the church on a different site within such burial ground, the Corporation shall re-convey to the Incumbent the freehold of the site required for such purpose.

Corporation may erect House for Keeper of Public Enclosure.

Section 206. The Corporation may, subject to the conditions of any grant, erect and maintain such house for the keeper of any Closed Burial Ground, and such public conveniences as the Corporation may from time to time think fit to provide.

Keys of Enclosure to be kept thereat.

Section 207. The Corporation, in the case of any such burial ground which they do not throw open to the public, shall cause the keys of such burial ground to be kept on some part thereof, or at some convenient place near thereto, and notice of the place of deposit shall be affixed to, upon, or near to the principal entrance to such burial ground; and every person who immediately before the commencement of this Act had, or whose personal representatives hereafter shall have, any right, privilege, or easement in respect of any vault, grave, tomb, tombstone, or monument therein, shall have access thereto at all reasonable times.

Power to Remove Tombstones in certain cases.

Section 208. In order that the Corporation may the better fence, level, lay out, turf, plant, embellish, and otherwise improve Closed Burial Grounds, they may, with the consent of the heirs or personal representatives of any person whose remains are interred therein, remove any tombstone or monument, and they may without such consent remove any such tombstone or monument if the inscription thereon shall have become illegible, or if upon diligent inquiry the Corporation shall be unable to find such heirs or personal representatives, provided that any such stone or monument so removed shall be placed in some other part of the Closed Burial Ground, and that a register be kept of the situation from and to which such stone or monument has been removed, and of such marks and signs as may aid in the future identification of the same.

Power to make Bye-laws.

Section 209. Subject to the conditions of any grant, the Corporation may from time to time make Bye-laws for all or any of the following purposes with respect to burial grounds over which they exercise rights under this Act (that is to say):

For the prevention of the posting of bills or placards, and the writing, stamping, cutting, printing, drawing, or marking in any manner of any word or character, or of any representation of any object, on any building, erection, monument, tombstone, wall, gate, door, railing, fence, tree, lamp-post, walk, pavement, or seat, or elsewhere in the enclosure.

For the preservation of order and good conduct among persons frequenting the enclosure.

For regulating the days and times of admission thereto.

For the prevention or restraint of acts or things tending to the injury or disfigurement of the enclosure or the fences thereof, or anything in or on the same or belonging thereto, or which may interfere with the use thereof by the public.

For preventing or regulating the admission of dogs.

For the removal of any person infringing any such bye-laws.

Appointment of Keepers and Servants.

Section 210. The Corporation may from time to time appoint, employ, and remove keepers and servants for such burial grounds, and they may make orders and regulations with respect to the salaries, wages, duties, and conduct of such keepers and servants.

Power to Corporation to bring Actions in respect of Injury to Burial Grounds.

Section 211. The Corporation may from time to time, in their own name, prosecute or defend any legal proceedings for recovering or defending the possession, for the purposes of this Act, or for obtaining the payment of damages, or any mandamus or injunction in respect of or against any actual or contemplated injury or damage to such burial grounds, or any part or parts thereof, or the fences, walks, graves, tombstones, and property in or about the same.

Damage to Public Enclosure, etc., to be paid for.

Section 212. The Corporation may, notwithstanding the infliction of a penalty, and in addition thereto, recover, either by action or summarily, from any person who does or causes to be done any injury to such burial ground, or the walls, rails, or fences thereof, or anything contained therein or thereon, the amount of the damage sustained by the Corporation by reason of such injury.

Purposes of part of Act—Sanitary Purposes.

Section 213. The purposes of this part of this Act shall be deemed to be sanitary purposes within the meaning of The Public Health Act, 1875.

Right of Clerks and Sextons to receive certain Fees to cease on Death of present holders of office.

Section 214. The right of every parish clerk and sexton to perform and exercise duties and functions, in respect of the burial of the remains of parishioners or inhabitants of the parish of which he is clerk or sexton, in any burial ground provided by the Burial Board for the Borough, under the provision of the Burial Acts, or to which this Act applies, and to receive fees on such burials, shall cease on the death of the present holders of these offices respectively; and no successor in office of any such parish clerk or sexton shall be entitled to perform or exercise any duties or functions, or to receive any fees, in respect of any burials in any such burial ground.

Saving rights of heirs, etc., of persons interred in burial grounds.

Section 215. Nothing in this part of this Act shall prejudice or interfere with the rights, privileges, or easements which any person immediately before the commencement of this Act had, or which his heirs or personal representatives may hereafter have, in respect of any vault, grave, tomb, tombstone, or monument, or the maintenance thereof, or the access thereto respectively, in any of the burial grounds to which this Act applies.

Saving of Liabilities.

Section 216. Nothing in this part of this Act shall exempt any person from any liability or obligation not otherwise expressly provided for by or under the provisions of this part of this Act.

Saving of other powers of Corporation.

Section 217. Nothing in this part of this Act shall deprive the Corporation, as the Sanitary Authority, or as the Burial Board, or otherwise, of any powers or authorities under any other general or local Act.

Copy of the Bye-laws and Regulations for the Management of the several Public Parks and Gardens, and the Closed Burial Grounds of the City, made by the Council in respect thereto.

CITY OF BIRMINGHAM.

PUBLIC PARKS.

At an adjourned Quarterly Meeting of the Council of this Borough, held pursuant to a resolution of the Council fixing the same, and to notice by the Mayor, on Tuesday, the 14th day of November, 1876, at Two o'clock in the afternoon, in the Council Chamber, at the Public Office in Moor Street:

Resolved—

10,576. That the following Code of Bye-laws and Regulations, in relation to the several Public Parks of the Corporation, be approved and adopted; and that the Baths and Parks Committee do take all necessary steps, in the name and on behalf of the Council, and under the Corporate Common Seal, for the purpose of complying with the provisions of "The Birmingham Parks Act, 1854," in reference to the making of Bye-laws and Regulations.

Whereas, by virtue of "The Birmingham Parks Act, 1854," the Council of the said Borough are empowered to make such Bye-laws and Regulations as they may think expedient for the purpose of carrying into effect the objects of the said Act, and to annex reasonable penalties for the breach of such Bye-laws and Regulations, or any of them.

Now we, the Council of the said Borough, at a meeting duly held this 14th day of November, 1876, at which at least two-thirds of the whole number of the Council were present, do make the following Bye-laws and Regulations for the management of the several Public Parks of the Borough.

GENERAL BYE-LAWS AND REGULATIONS APPLICABLE TO ALL THE PARKS.

The Parks shall be open to the public from six o'clock in the morning until sunset, between the 31st March and 30th September, and at other times between sunrise and sunset, except when otherwise specially provided.

A notice stating the time of closing shall be affixed at or near each of the entrances to the Parks; and all visitors shall leave the Parks at the time specified in such notice.

The Council may close any of the Parks, wholly or in part, on any days in the year, not exceeding seven days in the whole, and (unless prohibited by the conditions of the grant) may charge, or permit any person or persons to whom the use of the Park may have been given, to charge for admission on any of such days such sum or sums as the Council may prescribe or approve. The Council shall give at least three days' notice by advertisement, in one or more of the Birmingham newspapers, in every case of their intention to close the Parks, or any of them.

Horses and carriages will be permitted to enter the Parks where carriage drives are specially provided; but no horse or carriage shall be permitted to halt or loiter so as to impede the passage along the drives.

No person shall ride or drive furiously, so as to endanger the safety or convenience of any person, or to injure the Park.

No groom or horsebreaker shall exercise or train any horse in any part of the Parks.

The Council reserve the right to temporarily close the carriage drives for the purpose of repairs, or for any other special reason.

Chairs on wheels moved by hand, with invalids or children, shall be permitted to enter and remain in the Parks; but Bicycles, Velocipedes, Wheelbarrows, and Trucks, shall be excluded.

No dog shall be permitted to enter or remain in the Parks unless led by a cord, strap, or chain; nor shall any dog be put into or allowed to swim in any water in the Parks.

No person shall play at Cricket, Bowls, Bandy, Quoits, Rounders, Football, or any other game, except in such parts of the Parks as may be set apart for the purpose.

No intoxicated person shall be allowed to enter or remain in the Parks.

Profane, indecent, offensive, or insulting language or behaviour, gambling, and soliciting alms, are strictly forbidden.

No refreshments of any kind shall be hawked or sold in the Parks, except in the rooms, buildings, or places set apart for the purpose, and by persons duly authorised by the Council; and no intoxicating liquors shall be sold or consumed in the refreshment rooms or elsewhere in the Parks.

No person shall smoke in any building in the Parks.

Bands of music shall be allowed to play in the Parks on such days (Sundays excepted), in such situations, and subject to such conditions, as may be fixed by the Council; but no band shall play in the Parks until the permission of the Council shall have been obtained.

No person shall walk upon any flower bed, border, shrubbery, or plantation, or get over any fence, in any of the Parks.

No person shall go or remain in any part of the Parks where a notice is placed forbidding its use.

No person shall do any damage to any of the buildings, walks, fences, trees, shrubs, plants, or other property within the Parks; nor pluck any flower, or cut or break any tree or shrub therein.

No person shall capture any bird, nor take or disturb any bird's nest.

No preaching, lecture, or public discussion on any subject, and no meeting for the purpose of making any political or religious demonstration, or of holding any religious service, shall be allowed in the Parks.

No person shall bathe in any water in the Parks, except in such as shall be specially reserved for the purpose, and in that water only during such times, and subject to such regulations, as the Council may prescribe.

Hawkers and pedlars will not be allowed to ply their trades in the Parks.

No person shall discharge any fire-arm, or wantonly throw or discharge any stone or other missile, or make any bonfire, or (except with the consent of the Council) throw or set fire to any fireworks in the Parks.

No person shall wilfully interfere with or annoy any other person lawfully using the Parks in accordance with the Bye-laws.

No person shall wilfully disturb, worry, or illtreat any animal, waterfowl, or fish, in the Parks, or in the waters thereof.

No person shall, without permission of the Council, fish in any waters in the Parks.

On the ringing of the bell, all persons must forthwith leave the Parks.

C

SPECIAL BYE-LAWS AND REGULATIONS FOR CANNON HILL PARK.

No person shall use the Bathing Pond, the Boats upon the Lake, or the Gymnasium Ground, or Implements, except within such hours, and subject to such conditions, as may be prescribed by the Council of the Borough from time to time.

No person shall skate or slide in the Park, except with the consent and under the control of the Park-keeper.

All persons guilty of any breach of the Bye-laws will be liable to be at once removed from the Park.

No person shall resist a Constable or other servant of the Council in the discharge of his duties in the Park.

Any person offending against the above Bye-laws and Regulations, or any one of them, will be liable, on summary conviction, to a penalty not exceeding £5.

E. O. SMITH,

Town Clerk.

Corporate Seal.

REGULATIONS

FOR

REDNAL HILL AND BILBERRY HILL.

Anyone breaking or injuring any trees, shrubs, gates, fences, or other property, will be prosecuted.

Hawking of any description is strictly prohibited.

No fires are to be lighted without special permission.

Any person throwing stones, or using catapults or fire-arms, will be prosecuted.

Birds-nesting is strictly prohibited.

Any person taking any fern or root will be prosecuted.

Botanists and botanical parties must obtain permission from the Chairman of the Baths and Parks Committee before taking from the Hills specimen roots or ferns, or other plants.

No intoxicated person shall be allowed to remain on the Hills.

No Band shall play on the Hills until the permission of the Committee shall have been obtained.

No preaching, lecture, or public discussion on any subject, and no meeting for the purpose of making any political or religious demonstration, or of holding any religious service, shall be allowed on the Hills.

The public are respectfully requested to assist the keeper in the enforcement of the above Rules.

By order of the Baths and Parks Committee,

S. HEARN,
Superintendent Public Parks.

J. COX,
Secretary Parks Department.

CITY OF BIRMINGHAM.

CLOSED BURIAL GROUNDS.

BYE-LAWS

Made by the Council of the said Borough with respect to the Closed Burial Ground of the Church of Saint Martin, the Park Street Burial Grounds, the Closed Burial Ground of the Church of Saint Bartholomew, and the Closed Burial Ground of the Church of Saint Mary, in the said Borough.

At a Meeting of the Council of this Borough, held pursuant to a Resolution of the Council fixing the same, and to notice by the Mayor, on Tuesday, the 4th day of April, 1882, in the Council Chamber, at the Council House:

It was Resolved—

That the following Bye-laws, made pursuant to "The Birmingham Closed Burial Grounds Act, 1878," with respect to the several Closed Burial Grounds hereinafter specified, that is to say, the Closed Burial Ground of the Church of Saint Martin, the Closed Burial Grounds commonly known as the Park Street Burial Grounds, the Closed Burial Ground of the Church of Saint Bartholomew, and the Closed Burial Ground of the Church of Saint Mary, be and they are hereby approved and adopted; and that the Baths and Parks Committee do take all necessary steps, in the name and on behalf of the Council, and under the Corporate Common Seal, for the purpose of complying with the provisions of the said Act with reference to the making of Bye-laws.

CITY OF BIRMINGHAM.

CLOSED BURIAL GROUNDS.

Bye-laws made by the Mayor, Aldermen, and Burgesses of the Borough of Birmingham, acting by the Council, pursuant to " The Birmingham Closed Burial Grounds Act, 1878 " (41 Vict., c. 42), with respect to the several Closed Burial Grounds hereinafter specified, that is to say, the Closed Burial Ground of the Church of Saint Martin, the Closed Burial Grounds commonly known as the Park Street Burial Grounds, the Closed Burial Ground of the Church of Saint Bartholomew, and the Closed Burial Ground of the Church of Saint Mary, in the said Borough.

1. Every burial ground shall be open to the public from six o'clock in the morning until sunset on every day during the period between the 31st day of March and 30th day of September, both days inclusive, and from sunrise to sunset on every day during the period between the 1st day of October and the 30th day of March, both days inclusive.

2. A person other than an officer of the Corporation, or a person, or a servant of a person, employed by the Corporation in or about any work in connection with a burial ground, shall not on any day enter the burial ground before the time hereinbefore appointed for the opening thereof, or enter the burial ground, or remain therein, after the time hereinbefore appointed for the closing thereof.

3. A person other than an officer of the Corporation, or a person, or a servant of a person, employed by the Corporation in or about any work in connection with a burial ground, shall not at any time drive or wheel, or cause or suffer to be driven or wheeled, into the burial ground of any barrow, truck, bicycle, tricycle, velocipede, or any machine or vehicle other than a wheeled chair, perambulator, or chaise, drawn or propelled by hand, and used solely for the conveyance of invalids or children.

4. A person shall not cause or suffer any dog belonging to him, or in his charge, to enter or remain in a burial ground, unless such dog be, and continue to be, under proper control, and be effectually restrained from damaging such burial ground, or any grass, trees, shrubs, plants, or walks therein, and from causing annoyance to any person.

5. A person shall not play at cricket, bowls, bandy, quoits, rounders, football, or any other game in a burial ground.

6. A person shall not, in a burial ground, sell, or offer or expose for sale, or let to hire, or expose for letting to hire, any commodity or article, except in the rooms, buildings, or places set apart by the Council for the purpose, and in accordance with the terms of any agreement between such person and the Council.

7. A person shall not smoke tobacco, or other like substance, in any building in a burial ground.

8. A person shall not play upon any musical instrument, or take part in any musical or other entertainment, in the Closed Burial Grounds of the Churches of Saint Mary and Saint Bartholomew respectively.

A person shall not, except as is hereinafter provided, play upon any musical instrument, or take part in any musical entertainment, in the Closed Burial Ground of the Church of Saint Martin, and the Closed Burial Grounds commonly known as the Park Street Burial Grounds.

Provided that the foregoing prohibition shall not apply in any case where, upon an application to the Council for permission to play upon a musical instrument, or to take part in a musical entertainment, the Council may grant, subject to compliance with such conditions as they may prescribe, permission to any person to play upon such musical instrument, or to take part in such musical entertainment, in the Closed Burial Ground of the Church of Saint Martin, or in the Closed Burial Grounds commonly known as the Park Street Burial Grounds.

9. A person shall not walk upon any flower bed or border, or in any shrubbery or plantation, or climb any fence in or enclosing a burial ground.

10. A person other than an officer of the Corporation, or a person, or a servant of a person, employed by the Corporation in or about any work in connection with a burial ground, shall not enter upon any part of the ground which may be described in a notice or notices affixed or set up in such part, and may therein be declared to be closed for the time therein specified.

11. A person shall not carelessly or negligently injure or destroy any part of any fence in or enclosing a burial ground, or any part of any building, barrier, or railing, or of any fixed or movable seat, or of any other structure or erection, or of any walk in the burial ground.

12. A person shall not pluck any bud, blossom, flower, or leaf of any tree, sapling, shrub, or plant in a burial ground.

13. A person shall not take, injure, or destroy any bird, or take or disturb any bird's nest in a burial ground.

14. A person shall not preach or lecture, or take part in any public discussion on any subject, or hold or take part in any meeting for the purpose of making any political, religious, or other demonstration, or of holding any religious service in a burial ground.

15. A person shall not discharge any fire-arms, or wantonly throw or discharge any stone or other missile, or make or kindle any bonfire in a burial ground.

16. A person shall not wilfully obstruct, disturb, interrupt, or annoy any other person in the proper use of a burial ground, or wilfully obstruct, disturb, or interrupt any officer of the Town Council in the proper execution of his duty in the burial ground.

17. A person shall not wilfully disturb, worry, or ill-treat any animal in a burial ground.

18. A person shall not post a bill or placard on any building, erection, monument, tombstone, wall, gate, door, railing, fence, tree, lamp-post, walk, pavement, or elsewhere in a burial ground.

19. A person shall not write, stamp, cut, print, draw, or mark in any manner any word or character, or any representation of any object, on any building, erection, monument, tombstone, wall, gate, door, fence, tree, lamp-post, walk, pavement, or seat, or elsewhere in a burial ground.

20. Every person who offends against any of the foregoing Bye-laws shall be liable for every such offence to a penalty of Five Pounds.

Provided, nevertheless, that the Justices or Court before whom any complaint may be made, or any proceedings may be taken, in respect of any such offence, may, if they think fit, adjudge the payment as a penalty of any sum less than the full amount of the penalty imposed by this Bye-law.

21. Every person who in a burial ground infringes any of the foregoing Bye-laws may be removed from the burial ground by an officer of the Town Council, or by a constable, in any one of the several cases hereinafter specified (that is to say):

(i) Where the infraction of the Bye-law is committed within the view of such officer or constable, and the name and residence of the person infringing the Bye-law are unknown to, and cannot be readily ascertained by, such officer or constable:

(ii) Where the infraction of the Bye-law is committed within the view of such officer or constable, and from the nature of such infraction, or from any other fact of which such officer or constable may have knowledge, or of which he may be credibly informed, there may be reasonable ground for belief that the continuance in the burial ground of the person infringing the Bye-law may result in another infraction of a Bye-law, or that the removal of such person from the burial ground is otherwise necessary as a security for the proper use and regulation thereof.

E. O. SMITH,

Town Clerk.

Allowed by the Local Government Board this Twenty-seventh day of May, 1882.

J. G. DODSON,

President.

JOHN LAMBERT,
Secretary.

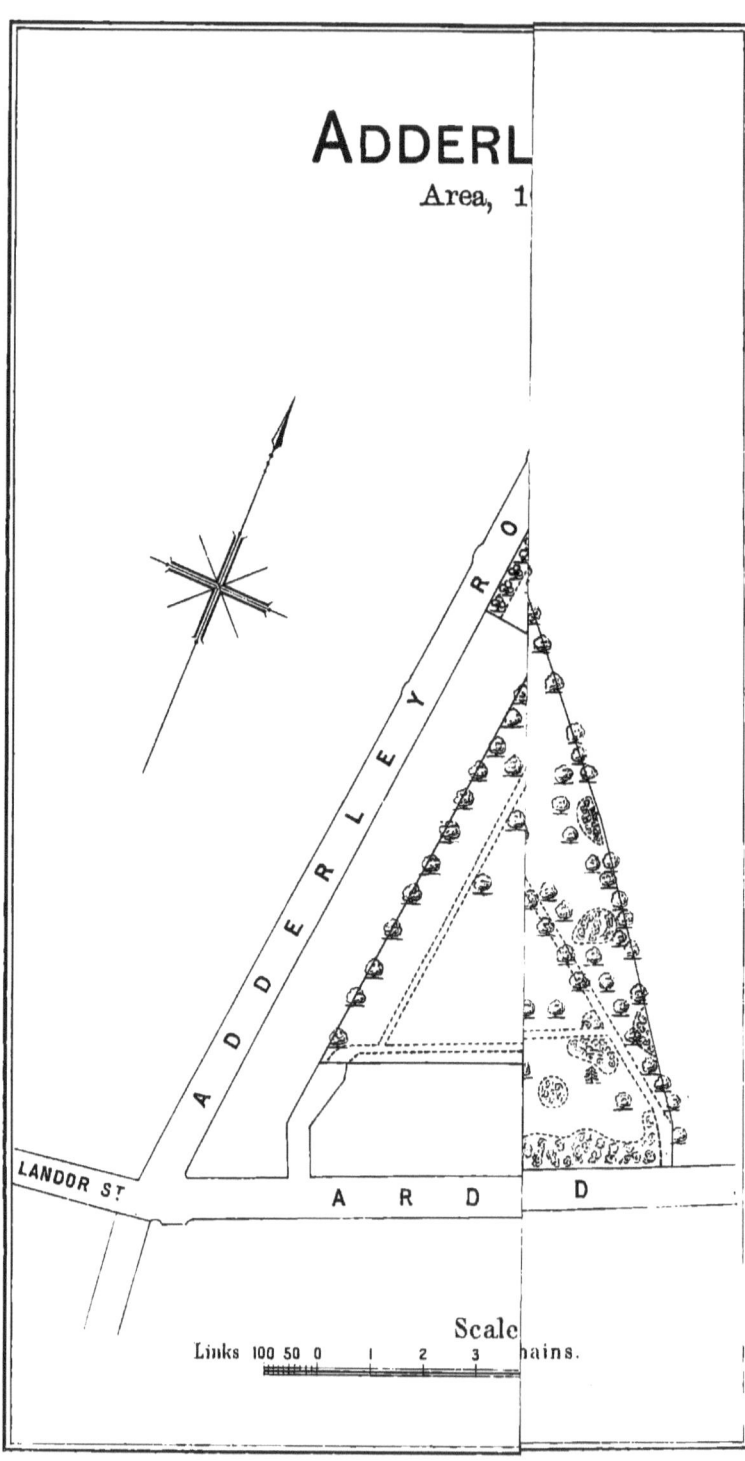

The following is a brief description of the various Parks and Pleasure Grounds belonging to the City of Birmingham, and of the manner of their acquirement by the Corporation.

ADDERLEY PARK.

This Park is situated on the east side of the city, and by the annexation of Saltley is now included within its boundaries. In the year 1855, Mr. Charles Bowyer Adderley, now Lord Norton, offered this land to the Town Council for use as a Public Park, on condition that the Council should lay out the Park in a proper manner, and permit the donor to have a share in its control, and a voice in the regulations relating thereto. These conditions being objected to, the offer was declined by the Town Council on the recommendation of the General Purposes Committee, to whom the subject had been referred. On the 23rd of August, 1855, Mr. Adderley wrote, stating that the Committee appeared to have misunderstood his offer, which practically amounted to a free gift of the land; but, lest the public should be deprived of an expected place of recreation, he would himself set apart the space for public use, and for the purpose of a playground for all classes of the people.

The Corporation did, however, subsequently accept Mr. Adderley's generous offer, but in a modified form, and a lease was entered into for a period of 999 years, at a peppercorn rent of 5s. per annum.

The Park was completed and opened on the 30th of August, 1856, during the mayoralty of Thomas R. Hodgson, Esq., the event being celebrated by a dinner held in a marquee erected in the Park, and at which upwards of 400 guests sat down.

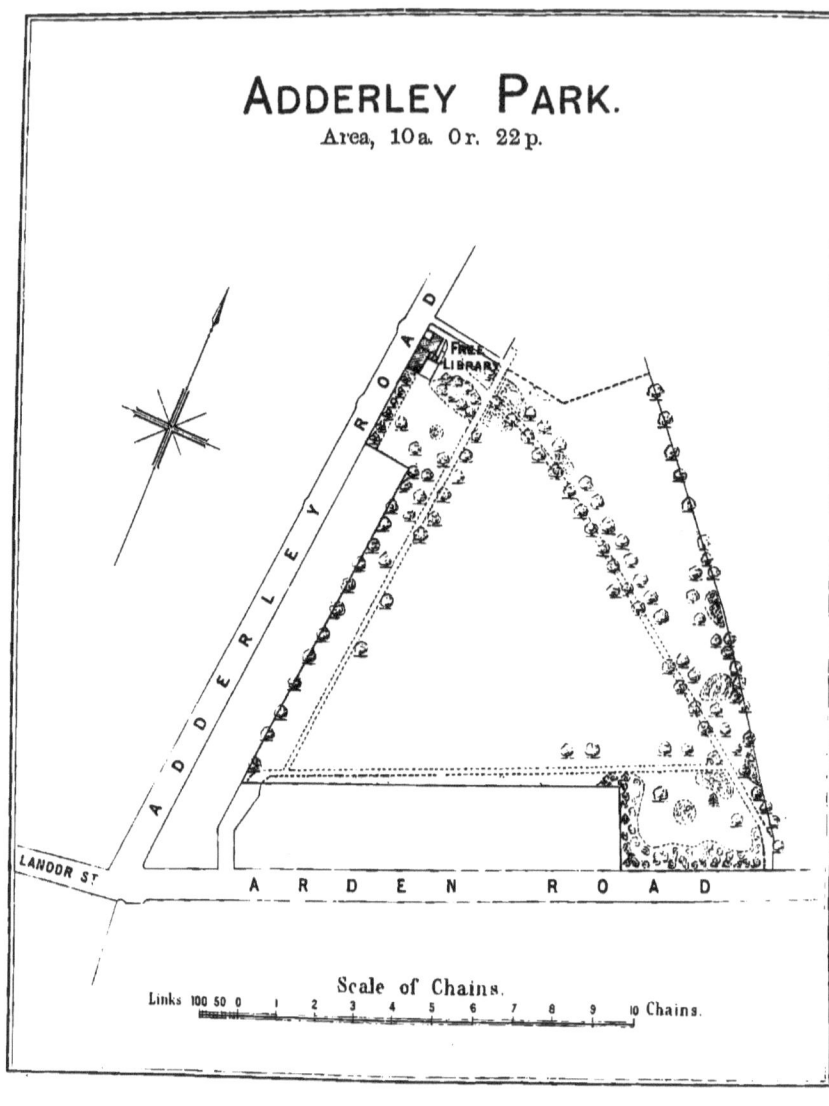

To further commemorate Mr. Adderley's generosity, the Council resolved, on the 9th day of December, 1862, to erect a suitable and imperishable monument, which took the form of a portrait of the donor, painted by Weigall, and deposited in the Corporation Art Gallery.

The total area of this Park is about 10a. 0r. 22p., of which about 2 acres are laid out and planted with shrubberies, flower beds, and suitable walks, the remainder being thrown open for general use as a playground, etc. The actual cost of maintenance is about £120 a year, including rates and taxes, and Park-keeper's wages, etc.

The building fronting the Park was erected by subscription, promoted by Mr. Adderley. It was originally used as a Museum and Reading Room, but subsequently the Museum was transferred to Aston Hall, and the building placed under the management of the Free Libraries Committee, and is now used as a Branch Free Library, in connection with the Central Library in Ratcliff Place.

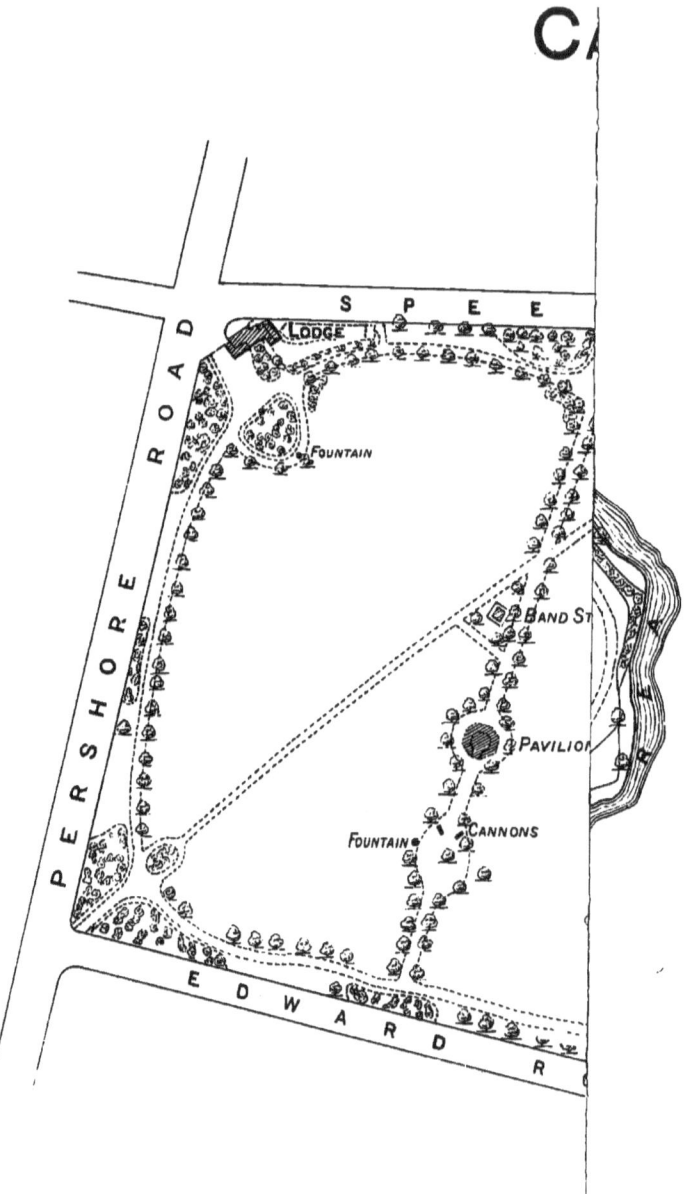

CALTHORPE PARK.

On the 1st of April, 1856, the General Purposes Committee presented a report to the Council, embodying an offer from Lord Calthorpe for letting to the Corporation a piece of land in the Pershore Road, and containing from 20 to 30 acres, for the purpose of public recreation, by way of experiment, for one year, at a rental of £3 per acre. This offer was accompanied by the following conditions:

1st. That the working classes shall have free admittance at all hours of the day during the six working days.

2nd. That no person shall be admitted on the ground on Sunday.

3rd. That all gambling, indecent language, and disorderly conduct be strictly prohibited.

4th. That no wine, malt liquor, or spirituous liquor be sold or consumed on the ground.

5th. That no smoking be allowed.

6th. That no horses and carriages be permitted to enter the grounds, except chairs on wheels with invalids and children.

7th. That no dogs be allowed to enter.

8th. That no games be allowed except cricket, rounders, trap ball, battledore, quoits, gymnastics, and archery.

9th. That bathing be prohibited.

10th. That Sunday and day-school children be admitted on the days of their anniversary.

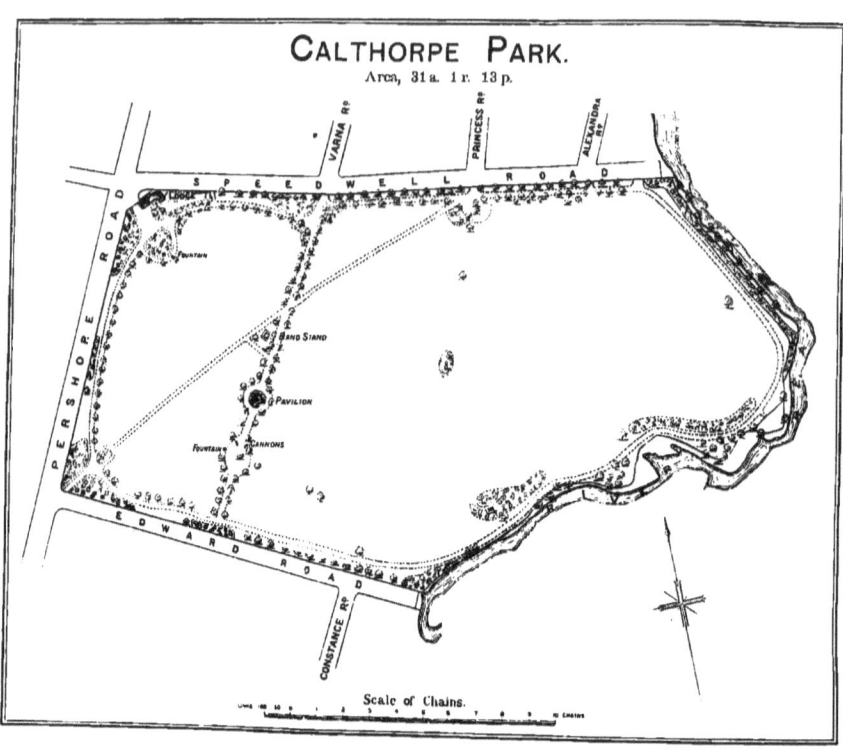

11th. That a proper number of police officers be in attendance, strictly to enforce the above regulations.

12th. That the fences be preserved from injury.

These proposals were considerably modified at the request of the Council, and the offer ultimately accepted, subject to the conditions referred to hereafter.

The Park was formally opened by His Royal Highness the Duke of Cambridge on the 1st day of June, 1857, and during the mayoralty of Sir John Ratcliff, the Duke being the guest of the Mayor on the occasion.

To commemorate the event, three trees of the " Cedrus Deodara" were planted in the centre of the Park—one by the Duke of Cambridge, one by Lord Calthorpe, and one by the Mayor.

Two guns captured from the Russians during the Crimean War were sent down by the Government as ornaments for the Park, and these were placed in the middle of the grounds, mounted on their original wood carriages. These carriages were removed in 1887, owing to their dilapidated and unsafe condition.

This Park is situated on the south side of the Borough, in St. Martin's Ward, and is divided from Balsall Heath Ward by the river Rea, which flows past a portion of the west and the whole of the southern boundary of the Park. It has a frontage to Pershore Road of about 400 yards, and is bounded on the east side by Speedwell Road, and on the west by Edward Road. The total area of the Park is about 31 acres 1 rood 13 perches, and for several years was maintained as an open playground. Many improvements in planting and new paths have of late years been made: a new Lodge, used as a Park-keeper's residence, has also been erected at the north-east corner of the Park, in conjunction with the handsome entrance gates and ornamental iron palisading running the full length of the Pershore Road frontage; the east and west boundaries are also protected by strong oak cleft railing, about 5 ft. 6 in. high.

A large refreshment room has been erected in the centre of the Park, and constructed with an octagonal roof overhanging the walls some nine or ten feet, forming a shelter on all sides during wet weather. About five acres of the grounds, principally near the Pershore Road frontage, has recently been laid out with flower beds and shrubberies; but the greater portion is still open for the free use of the public, and it continues, as it always has been, a favourite place of resort for cricket and football clubs, and during a portion of the year it is used as an exercising ground by the Rifle Volunteers, subject to the permission of the Baths and Parks Committee, which is applied for annually.

The tenure of Calthorpe Park has been the subject of considerable negotiation. The Town Council became occupiers by permission of Lord Calthorpe in 1857, but not under any legal document. They were therefore occupiers on sufferance, on payment of a nominal rent of £5. Lord Calthorpe offered to grant a perpetual lease to the Council at a nominal rent, but in consequence of his son being out of England nothing was done in the matter until the 30th day of April, 1862, when a deputation waited upon his Lordship on the subject. Lord Calthorpe declined then to enter into any legal agreement, stating that he had not been consulted as to the proposal for a perpetual lease; and up to his death, which occurred on the 2nd of May, 1868, the occupation on sufferance continued.

In 1870, negotiations were opened with the present Lord Calthorpe, when, in a letter from his solicitor, dated May 23rd, an offer was made to grant a lease of the land for 21 years— the longest term, as a life-holder, he had power to give—the rent to be fixed at £300 per annum, with an honourable understanding on his part that £295 should be returned to the Council. This offer the Council declined, as it would not have justified them in any expenditure on the Park; and the Baths and Parks Committee were thereupon instructed by the Council to seek an interview with Lord Calthorpe, with the result that on the 22nd of August, 1871, they reported to the Council that the grant of the Park to the Corporation had been executed by Lord Calthorpe, and also by his lordship's brothers, The Hon. Augustus Calthorpe and The Hon. Somerset

Calthorpe; the deed had been duly enrolled in the Court of Chancery, and that, so far as they were individually able, Lord Calthorpe and his brothers divested themselves of all interest existing, or that might accrue thereon, in favour of the Corporation, as representatives of the borough.

The difficulties which arose as to the tenure of the Park were due to the state of the laws as to life-holders of land : a proprietor who holds merely for his life can grant a lease for no longer term than 21 years, and can let only at a fair annual value. This was the reason why Lord Calthorpe had to require a rent of £300, and why he could only enter into an honourable engagement to return the £295, and these restrictions were made for the sake of protecting the rights of the successors in title. They are overcome by the generous deed of renunciation exercised by the members of the Calthorpe family.

The annual cost of maintenance of the Park is about £350, including an expenditure of £150 for wages, £25 rates and taxes, and £4 11s. 6d. tithe rent charge.

There is an income of £30 a year derived from the letting of the refreshment room and grazing land, and this is supplemented by about £20 a year obtained from the charges made for cricket and football, etc.

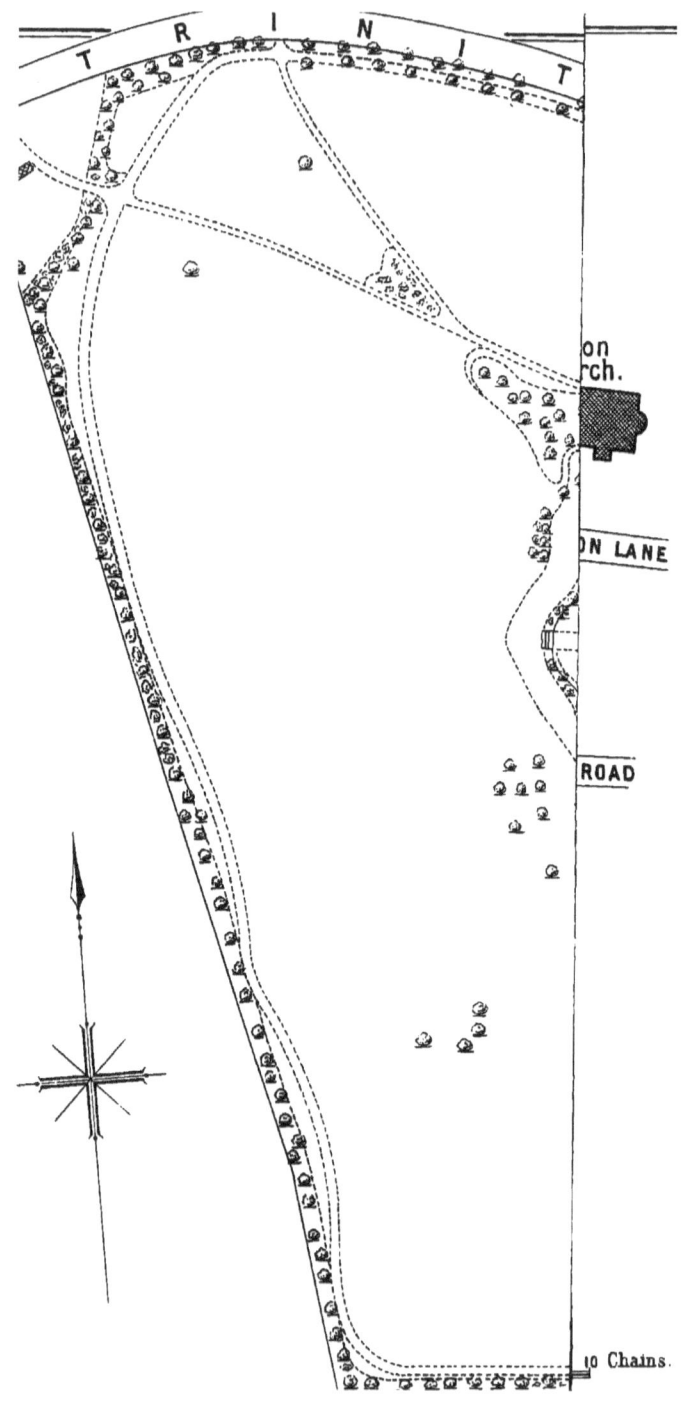

ASTON PARK,

Situated on the North-east side of the City, in the Manor of Aston, in the County of Warwick; distant about three miles from Stephenson Place, and can be reached either by steam tram cars leaving the Old Square, or by the London and North Western Railway to Aston or Witton Stations.

Aston Hall, which stands in the centre of the Park, was originally the seat of the Holte family; but for several years, early in the present century, was the residence of Mr. James Watt, son of the eminent engineer, and for a short time after the death of this gentleman it was occupied by the late Mr. James Shaw, and afterwards remained vacant for a considerable period. This building and the Museum contained therein is now under the care of the Museum and School of Art Committee.

The first reference to the purchase of this Park appears in the minutes of the Council for the 6th of August, 1850, when, at a Quarterly Meeting of the Council held on that day, the Mayor, Mr. William Lucy, informed the Council that he had received an offer of the Aston Park Estate, which contained about 170 acres, and which the proprietors valued at £150,000, and suggested the propriety of entering into a treaty for its purchase as a place of public recreation and amusement for the burgesses whom they represented. A committee was thereupon appointed to open a communication with the owners, Messrs. Greenway, Greaves, and Whitehead, bankers, of Warwick, with a view of obtaining the refusal of the purchase until the end of the next session of Parliament, the Council not having up to that date obtained any powers which would enable them to purchase the estate out of the rates of the Borough. On the 29th October following, the committee reported that Mr. Robbins, the agent, declined to enter into any treaty of the kind proposed, and consequently the matter was deferred for some considerable time.

D

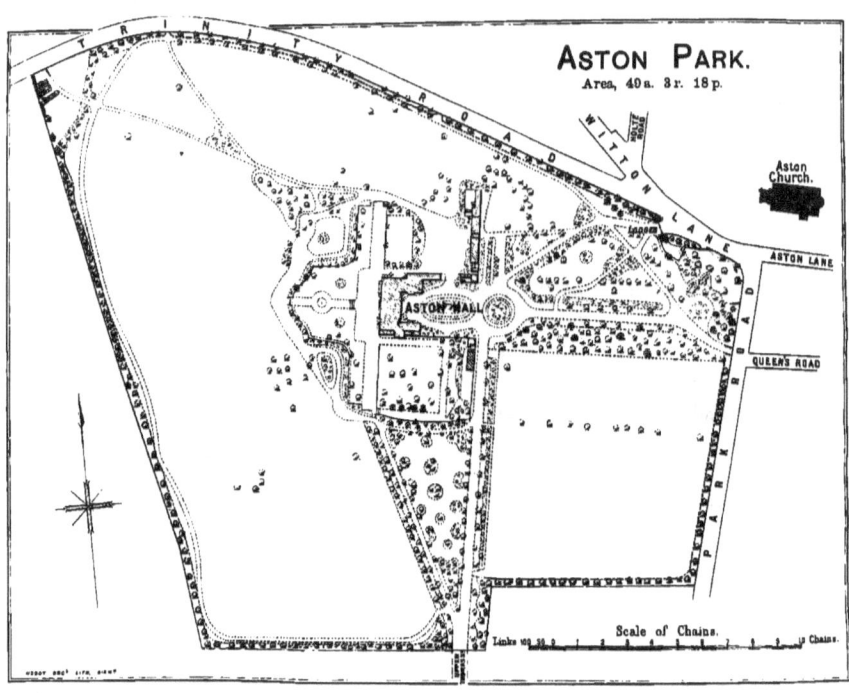

In 1854, an Act of Parliament was obtained which enabled the Council to purchase land for such purposes as those referred to, and was called

"THE BIRMINGHAM PARKS ACT."

On the 22nd August, 1856, the subject was again brought forward in the Council, and the Committee were instructed, in conjunction with the Borough Surveyor, to communicate with the owners, and ascertain the terms upon which the estate could be acquired, the result of which was reported to the Council on the 31st of October following, stating that they had instructed Mr. John L. Hornblower to select from Aston Park such an eligible portion as might be purchased for the sum of £30,000, including the Hall and buildings adjoining, and to submit a plan, with a report and full particulars thereon.

In reply, Mr. Hornblower selected about eighty-two acres of the land (including a large pool, now filled up), and immediately surrounding the Hall, as being specially suited to the requirements of a Public Park, and he valued the same at £23,000. The whole area of the estate at that time was from 160 to 170 acres, valued by Mr. Hornblower at £50,000. The proprietors had, however, set a much higher value upon the land, and estimated the selected eighty-two acres at £60,900; and a still narrower circle of land surrounding the Hall, containing about thirty acres, they valued at £24,500. To this sum the Council demurred, and instructed the Committee to ascertain if any reduction in the price could be obtained, and to report thereon, with such recommendations as they thought fit to make as to the extent of land they deemed it desirable to purchase, and the price which should be given by the Council for the same. The proprietors, however, declined to make any reduction or abatement whatever, as they considered the land alone to be worth the sum mentioned, the Hall to be given into the bargain. Upon this being reported to the Council, on the 6th of January, 1857, the Committee were instructed to obtain particulars as to the areas and cost of Public Parks in other large towns, and from their report it was seen that while Birmingham was as yet without any Public Park, Nottingham had two, one of which was eighty acres in extent, and the other fifty acres; Leeds and Bradford had one each of sixty-two acres; Glasgow three, covering a total area of 300 acres; and Derby had one of sixteen acres.

Whilst the Council were thus hesitating as to the steps they should take, and the price which should be paid for the land, a Limited Liability Company was formed for the purchase of a portion of the estate, including the Hall, with a view to its conversion into a place of public recreation and amusement, on the model of the Crystal Palace at Sydenham, opened a few years previously. The object of the Company, as stated in their Memorandum of Association, was—

1st. To purchase the Park, etc., with a view to derive a profit from such purchase, and thereby to compensate the Company for outlay.

2nd. With ultimate intention, after providing such compensation, to appropriate the Hall and premises to the use of the public, so far as to admit the public thereto, and to apply all profits to the maintenance and improvement of the Hall and premises, and not for any pecuniary benefit of the company of shareholders.

The purchase money for the Hall and 43 acres of land amounted to £35,000, and when the transfer was completed there was a universal desire that the Queen should be asked to open the Park in person, and that desire was conveyed by the Mayor, Mr. John Ratcliff, to the Earl of Shaftesbury by letter, dated March 6th, 1858, and in which the whole purpose of the acquisition of the estate was set forth, and describing the beauties thereof, and the advantage to be derived by the inhabitants of Birmingham thereby. On the 15th day of April the Mayor received Her Majesty's reply, stating that she would be willing to visit Birmingham some day during the week beginning 13th June.

On the 27th April a special meeting of the Town Council was held, to receive a report from the General Purposes Committee as to the arrangements to be made for the reception of Her Majesty, and to consider the form of the address which was to be presented on the occasion. These were finally approved and adopted by the Council on the 7th day of June, and on the 15th of that month the inhabitants of Birmingham were honoured by the presence of their Sovereign and her illustrious Consort, who arrived at the New Street Station of the London and North Western Railway shortly after twelve o'clock. The Mayor and Town Clerk, in full official municipal costumes, were in attendance to receive and conduct their royal visitors to the Town Hall. Her Majesty and suite were escorted by a detachment of the 10th Hussars, the royal carriage being preceded by the carriage containing the Mayor and Town Clerk, with the Mayor's Chaplain. The procession passed through some of the principal streets to the Town Hall, and alighting at the front entrance thereto, in Paradise Street, the proceedings commenced with the singing of the National Anthem by the choir, after which addresses were presented to Her Majesty and to the Prince Consort by the Mayor, each address having been previously read by the Town Clerk. To these addresses Her Majesty and the Prince Consort made gracious and suitable replies; and at the conclusion of the Prince's reply, the Secretary of State communicated to the Mayor Her Majesty's commands for him to approach the throne. The Mayor having obeyed, Her Majesty, receiving a sword from her Equerry, conferred the honour of knighthood upon Mr. John Ratcliff. Mr. Alderman Hodgson and Mr. Alderman Palmer, the mover and seconder of the address to Her Majesty, and Mr. Alderman Phillips and Mr. Alderman Carter, the mover and seconder of the address to the Prince Consort, were severally presented to Her Majesty, and had the honour of kissing hands. The other members of the Council were then individually introduced to the Queen.

The Royal Party, accompanied by the Mayor, Town Clerk, the Members of the Town Council, City Magistrates, etc., proceeded to Aston Hall, when Her Majesty, after partaking of luncheon, received an address from the Interim Managers of the Aston Park Company, and then formally inaugurated the opening of the Hall and Park. At the conclusion of the ceremony, the Royal Party proceeded to the temporary railway station at Aston, from whence they took their departure;

previous to her departure, Her Majesty expressed to the Mayor her high gratification at the welcome she had received.

The Hall and Park thus opened became one of the most popular resorts in the Midland Counties, until the year 1863, when an unfortunate occurrence attended one of the performances provided by the Company, whereby a woman named Powell, and styling herself "Female Blondin," was killed instantaneously by the breaking of the rope upon which she was performing at a great height from the ground. A considerable amount of excitement and indignation was created that the Company should sanction such dangerous exhibitions, and this was heightened by a letter addressed to the Mayor by command of the Queen, in which Her Majesty expressed her personal disapproval of such an exhibition, and hoping that the Mayor, in common with the rest of her people, would use their influence to prevent such exhibitions in the Park which Her Majesty and the Prince Consort had been pleased to open, in the hope that it would be used for the healthy exercise and rational recreation of the people. This unfortunate occurrence was partly instrumental in bringing about the acquisition of the Hall and Park by the Town Council, for at the same meeting of the Council at which Her Majesty's letter was read, a copy of two resolutions, passed at a meeting of the Aston Park Company, was also received, informing the Council that, in the opinion of the managers, the recent calamity that occurred during the holding of a Foresters' fête in the Park would considerably increase the difficulties in securing the Hall and Park on the original plan of the Limited Liability Act, and therefore the Company were desirous that steps should be taken to arrange with the Corporation for the completion of the purchase, and requesting the Mayor to take such steps as he may deem advisable in reference thereto. As a result of this communication, the Mayor (Alderman Sturge) addressed a letter to the Lord Lieutenant of the County, Lord Leigh, stating that the Company would be unable to hold possession of the property much longer; and with a view of securing it for the use of the people, the Mayor suggested that, if the county would raise the sum of £8,000 towards its purchase, he would move the Town Council to vote £20,000 for completing the sum that was required to effect the purchase.

Lord Leigh, after consulting the magistrates of the county, declined to take any steps in the matter, and while the question was pending, a second letter, dated November 4th, 1863, was addressed to the Mayor by the Queen's Secretary, stating that Her Majesty was unwilling to believe there could be any difficulty in acquiring the Park for public use. The question was then brought before the Town Council on the 15th day of December, 1863, when the proposed purchase was rejected by 40 votes to 12. This led to a private subscription being raised in aid of the purchase, and a sum of £7,000 was contributed, £2,000 being given by Mr. George Dixon, and his brother, Mr. Abraham Dixon; £1,000 each were also given by Miss Ryland, Thomas Lloyd, Esq., and G. F. Muntz, Esq., and other amounts by the following donors: William Middlemore, Esq., £500; Richard Greaves, Esq., Edward Greaves, Esq., M.P., and Jeffry Berington Lowe, Esq., £500; Archibald and Timothy Kenrick, Esqs., £500; Sampson S. Lloyd and George Braithwaite Lloyd, Esqs., £200; Alfred and Douglas Evans, Esqs., £200; and Charles and James Shaw, Esqs., £100. As before stated, the total purchase-money was £35,000, and of this sum the Company had paid £9,000, leaving a balance of £26,000. This amount was now reduced to £19,000, and the Council, after receiving a deputation from the donors, agreed on the 2nd of February, 1864, to pay the balance, and purchase the property. The resolution for the purchase was met with three amendments, but was ultimately carried by 34 votes to 14.

The Company was formally wound up on the 7th August, 1866, and all the shareholders relinquished their claims thereto. The purchase was completed by the Corporation on the 12th of September, 1864, and on the 22nd of that month the Hall and Park were opened free to the public, for their use and enjoyment for ever, the event being celebrated by a banquet given in the long gallery of the Hall by Mr. W. Holliday, the Mayor. The total area of the Park, as purchased by the Corporation, was 43 acres; and in 1873 a field adjoining, containing about 6 acres, was purchased at a cost of £4,750, making a total area of the grounds at present about forty-nine and one quarter acres. About 15 acres of this land immediately surrounding the Hall is laid out with flower beds, tennis lawn and bowling green, and the remainder is devoted to the public for general recreation. In addition to the Park and Grounds, the company handed over to the Corporation a large number of interesting and valuable articles deposited in the different apartments of the hall, most of them having been presented by the various donors. The Company had also erected certain buildings, including a glass pavilion on the south side of the Hall, which cost upwards of £1,300; they also effected many improvements on the estate, at a total outlay of from £6,000 to £7,000.

Aston Hall was made use of for the exhibition of works of art, antiquities, and natural history collections, etc.; but with the opening of the New Art Gallery at the Council House the principal objects of interest were transferred to that building. Other attractions have, however, been added, including the allocation of an apartment known as the Johnson room, to commemorate the connection of Dr. Samuel Johnson with Birmingham. In 1883 a large portion of the wainscoting and other fittings of one of the rooms of a house in the Old Square where Dr. Johnson was a frequent visitor, and at one time occupied by his friend Mr. Edmund Hector, were removed, and re-fitted in this room, together with other Johnson relics presented at the same time.

The Hall was placed under the control and management of the Baths and Parks Committee until the year 1887, when, by resolution of the Council, on the 7th day of July, that building was transferred to the care of the Museum and School of Art Committee, the Park and outbuildings still remaining under the control of this Committee. In 1887, the glass pavilion previously referred to was taken down, and the materials disposed of, thus enabling the Committee to restore the original character and appearance of the south side of the Hall.

The principal entrance to the Park is from Church Road, through a gateway formerly used by the tenants of the Hall, and having a keeper's lodge on either side. These lodges are now occupied by workmen employed in the Park. A carriage drive leads from this gateway up rising ground direct to the front entrance of the mansion, and is continued round the four sides of the Park. On the west side of the Hall is the courtyard, with a large range of buildings once used as stabling and coach-houses; but, on the acquisition of the property by the Corporation, these buildings were re-constructed for the purpose of refreshment and tea rooms and domestic apartments for the use of the persons to whom these rooms were let. Further alterations were made to these buildings in 1890 by the construction of additional rooms for the accommodation of the head gardener, who had hitherto resided some distance from the Park.

The expense of maintaining the Hall and Park, in addition to the interest and sinking fund, was about £1,500 per annum. The cost of maintaining the Park only, since the transfer of the Hall to the Museum and School of Art Committee, is about £750 a year, including about £430 for wages, and £74 for rates and taxes. There is an income of £40 a year derived from the letting of the refreshment room, and from £20 to £25 from the charges made in connection with the various games played in the Park.

The total cost of the Park to the Corporation, including the purchase of the additional land, and for works of restoration, etc., was £26,750, borrowed for repayment during a term of fifty years. Of this amount, £12,188 8s. 4d. has been repaid up to the 31st March, 1891.

There are several glass houses erected in the Park, for the purpose of propagating plants used in the flower beds. The total area of these is about 313 square yards.

The staff consists of one Head Gardener, with seven assistant gardeners.

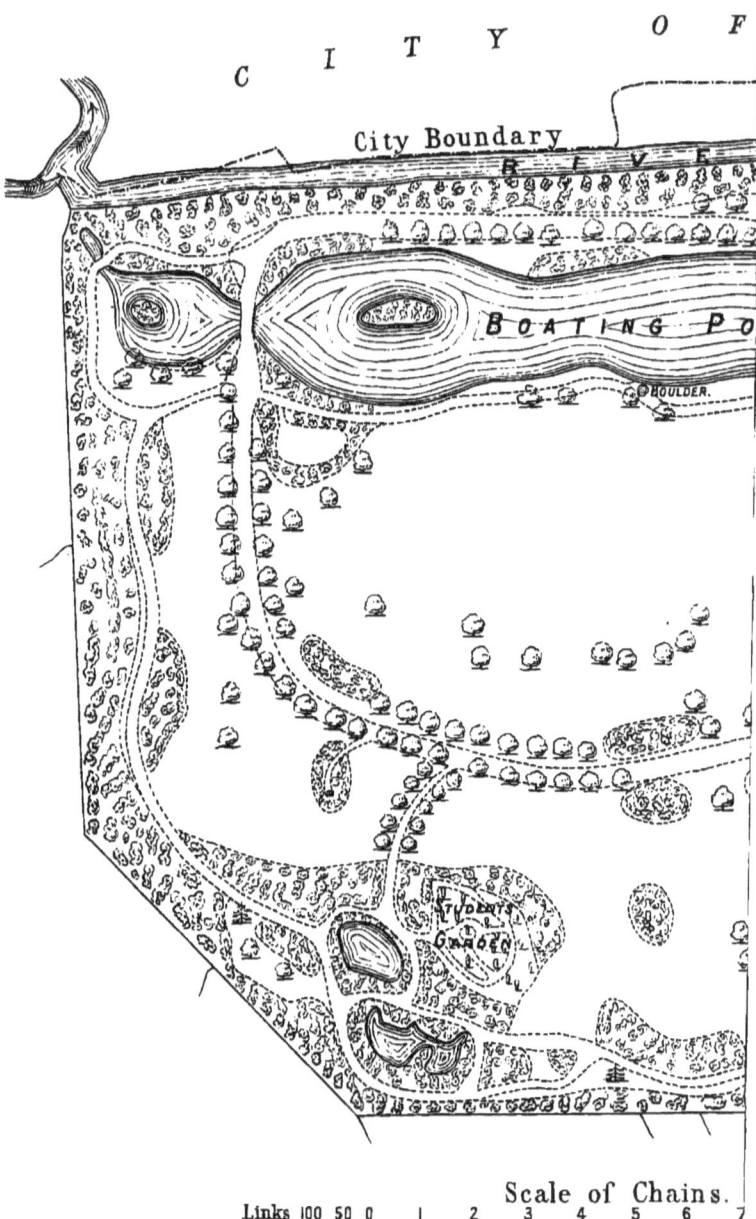

CANNON HILL PARK.

During the nine years following the acquisition of Aston Park, no addition was made to our Public Parks until 1873, when a fourth Park was contributed by the munificent generosity of Miss Louisa Ann Ryland, of Barford Hill, Warwickshire, the representative of an old Birmingham family.

The Park is situated on the south-west side of the City, just outside its newly-extended boundary, in the county of Worcester, and in the parish of Kings Norton. It is in close proximity to Calthorpe Park, and divided therefrom by one or two fields of pasture land on the opposite side of the river Rea. Before its presentation to the town, the grounds consisted of pasture land, on which grew some fine forest trees, but Miss Ryland most generously, at her own expense, caused it to be drained, laid out, and planted, so as to render it suitable for the purpose of a Park.

Mr. J. T. Gibson, of Battersea, was employed by Miss Ryland to execute the work, and under his direction about 35 acres were devoted to ornamental gardening, including shrubberies, etc., in which were planted many rare and choice trees, shrubs, and evergreens. Two large pools, surrounded with walks and plantations, were also constructed, with smaller ponds adjoining. The largest of these pools covers an area of about 15,000 square yards, and the other about 10,200 square yards : a suitable boathouse is erected between the two. On the north side of the Park a large bathing pool was constructed, and enclosed with high wood fencing and shrubs. This pool is about 216 feet in length by 100 feet in width, and has a depth varying from 2 feet 6 inches to 5 feet 6 inches. The bottom is formed of concrete, and water is supplied from a small stream which has its source within the boundaries of the Park. One long dressing-shed, divided

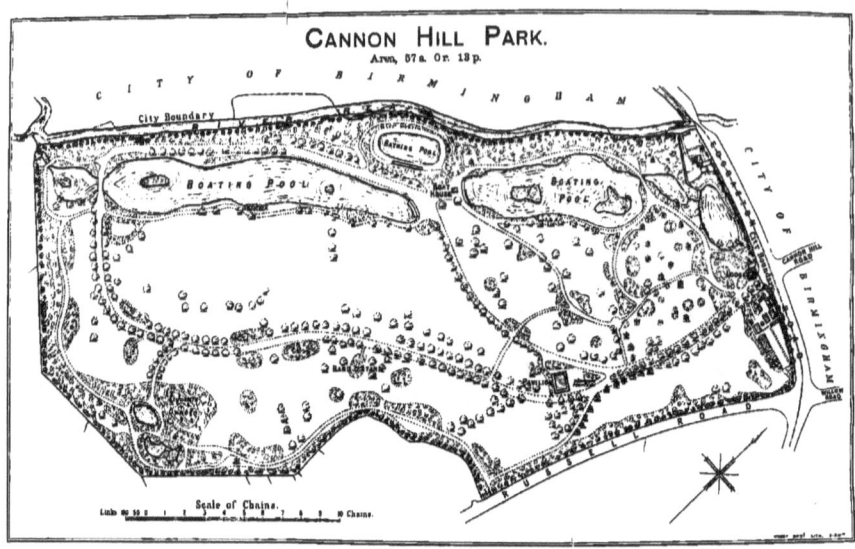

into several compartments, is erected on the south side of the pool, and is paved with blue bricks, the remaining portions of the promenade being formed of turf. The Bathing pool is let to the lessee of the Boating pool and Refreshment room, and the charge for admission is one penny. In addition to laying out of the Park and the formation of the Boating and Bathing pools, Miss Ryland provided a spacious ornamental pavilion, for use as a Refreshment room. This building is 45 feet in length by 25 feet in width, and the roof is specially constructed to form shelter on either side for the comfort and convenience of visitors thereto. The cost of erecting the picturesque building as a Park-keeper's lodge, with the principal entrance gates, and the cast-iron ornamental palisading on either side, was also defrayed by Miss Ryland, there being no expenditure incurred by the Corporation beyond the ordinary cost of maintenance and the erection of greenhouses, etc.

The Park was opened to the public on the 1st day of September, 1873, by Mr. Alderman Biggs (Mayor); but, by Miss Ryland's express desire, there was no ceremony on the occasion, and although the Corporation were most desirous that the Park should bear the name of the donor, Miss Ryland declined to assent to the request. To every visitor to the Park on the day of the opening was presented, as a memento of the occasion, a card bearing the following inscription:

"CANNON HILL PARK, OPENED 1ST SEPTEMBER, 1873.

"THROUGH THE BOUNTY OF GOD, I HAVE GREAT PLEASURE IN GIVING CANNON HILL PARK TO THE CORPORATION OF BIRMINGHAM, FOR THE USE OF THE PEOPLE OF THE TOWN AND NEIGHBOURHOOD. I WOULD EXPRESS MY EARNEST HOPE THAT THE PARK MAY PROVE A SOURCE OF HEALTHFUL RECREATION TO THE PEOPLE OF BIRMINGHAM, AND THAT THEY WILL AID IN THE PROTECTION AND PRESERVATION OF WHAT IS NOW THEIR OWN PROPERTY.
"LOUISA ANN RYLAND.
"BARFORD HILL, WARWICK."

The principal entrance to the Park is in Edgbaston Road, and the carriage drive therefrom is planted on either side with forest trees.

On the south-west corner of the Park a Students' Garden has been formed, for the special use of Botanical Students, and adjoining is a pleasant retreat called "The Fernery." Here is a small pond in which grow aquatic plants, and nearly every variety of English fern may be found on its banks. From this point a delightful view is obtained of the adjacent country.

For the purpose of propagating the various kinds of plants used in the extensive flower beds in this Park, and for supplying similar plants to the smaller parks and gardens of the city, six greenhouses have been erected near the Park-keeper's lodge, the whole having an area of about 435 square yards, including glass frames, etc.

The staff consists of one Park-keeper and nine gardeners (exclusive of the Parks Superintendent, who resides at the lodge). The Park-keeper and head gardener reside in two small cottages on a portion of the land included in Miss Ryland's gift, but situated outside of the Park boundary, and which was left undisturbed when the Park was laid out.

The annual cost of maintenance (exclusive of the Superintendent's salary) is about £1,100 per annum, including about £660 for wages, £60 rates and taxes, and £380 for general maintenance.

The following income is derived from various sources:

	£	s	d.
Rent of Refreshment Room premises...	60	0	0
,, Boating Pool	120	0	0
,, Bathing ,, ...	40	0	0
,, Grazing Land	35	0	0
Total	£255	0	0

To this must be added about £70 a year derived from the charges made for use of the various appliances provided by the Corporation, in connection with some of the games played in the Park, and from the sale of grass, hire of chairs, etc.

HIGHGATE PARK.
Area, 8 a. 3 r. 28 p.

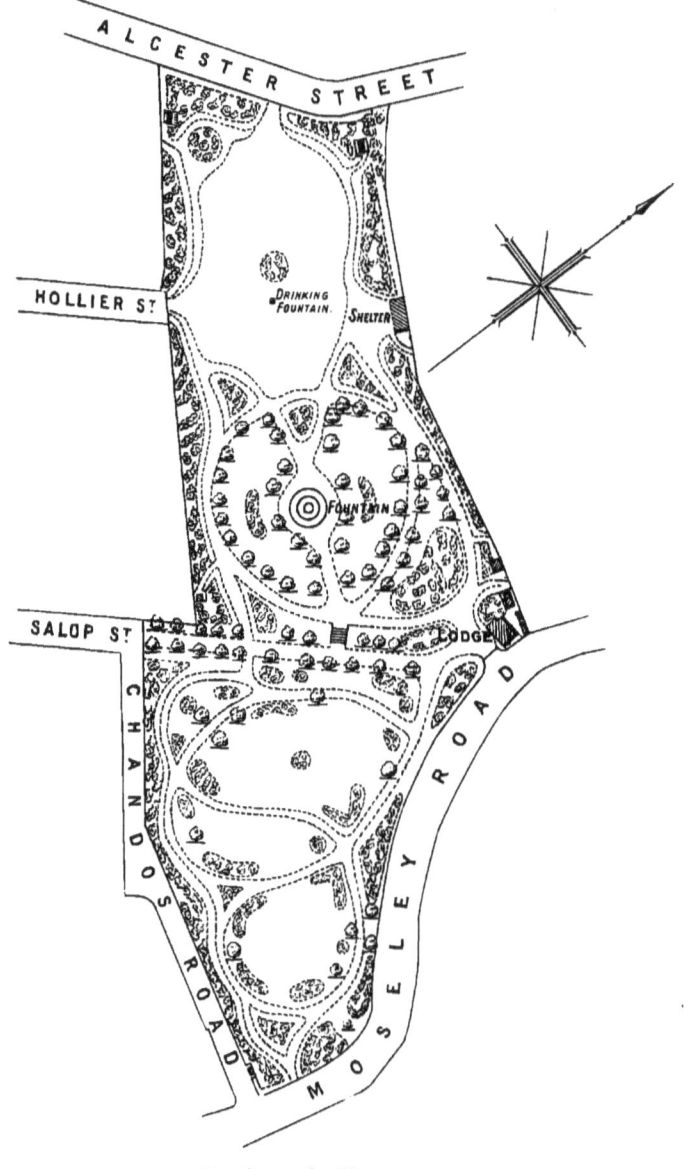

HIGHGATE PARK.

On the 25th of May, 1875, the Council sanctioned the purchase of the land for the formation of this Park, which is on the south-east side of the City, adjoining the Moseley Road, having an area of about 8a. 3r. 28p., with frontages to Moseley Road, Chandos Road, and Alcester Street, formerly known as "Hollier's Charity Land." The upper portion is tastefully laid out with ornamental flower beds, shrubberies, and well-kept lawn, and is divided from the lower part by a broad gravelled terrace, to which access is gained by means of two flights of wide stone steps.

About 5,445 square yards of the lower ground is covered with asphalte, to serve as a playground for the children living in that densely-populated neighbourhood.

The principal entrance is on the east side, near the Moseley Road, adjoining which is the Park-keeper's lodge; there are also other entrances from Moseley Road, Chandos Road, and Alcester Street.

The Park was opened by Joseph Chamberlain, Esq., Mayor, on the 2nd of June, 1876. The cost of the land was about £8,000, to which must be added £7,149 for laying out and fencing, etc., making a total expenditure of £15,149. This, however, was subsequently reduced by the sale of a portion of the land to the Birmingham School Board for £628. Another portion of the land, divided from the Park by Chandos Road, containing about 2,000 square yards, is reserved as a site for the erection of Public Baths thereon. The massive bronze fountain which for many years stood in the centre of the Market Hall was removed to this Park and formally opened by the then Mayor, Richard Chamberlain, Esq.

The annual cost of maintenance is about £350 a year, including about £200 for wages, £7 rates and taxes, and £3 for tithe rent charges.

The staff consists of one resident Park-keeper and three assistants

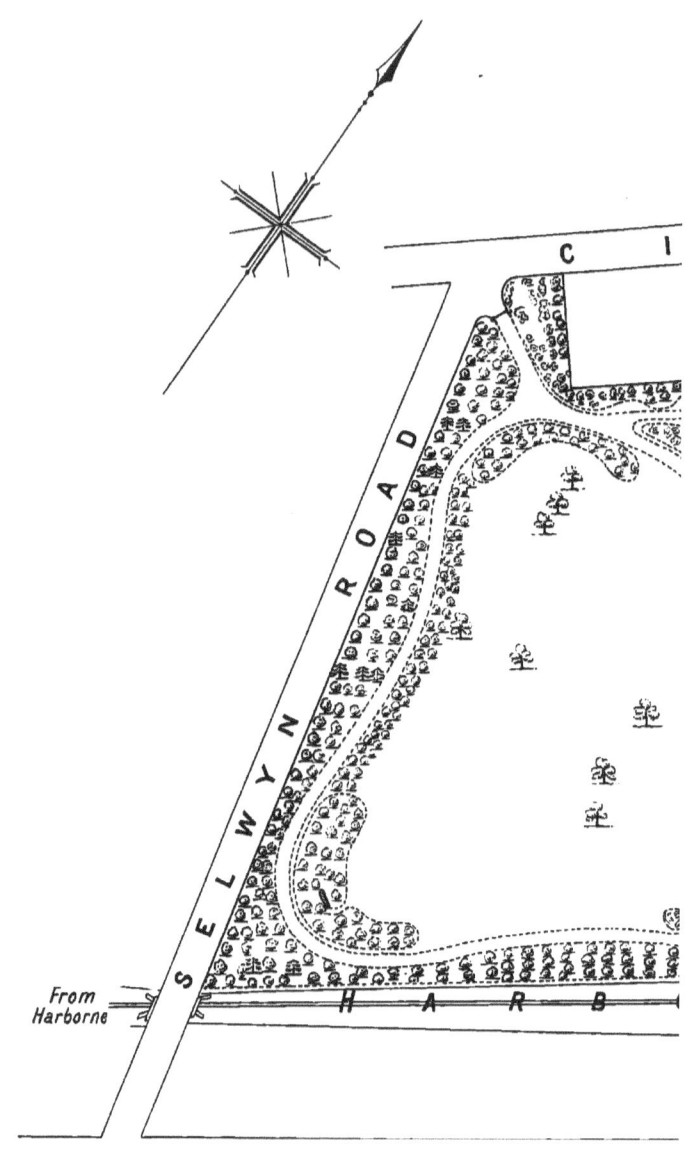

SUMMERFIELD PARK.

In the month following that of the opening of Highgate Park, Summerfield Park was also opened to the public. The opening ceremony was performed on the 29th day of July, 1876, by Mr. Alderman Baker, who had been elected to the mayoralty, on Mr. Joseph Chamberlain becoming a Member of Parliament for the Borough. The area of the Park at that time was a little over twelve acres, and was purchased by the Corporation for the sum of £8,000, including the mansion, for many years the residence of the late Mr. Lucas Chance, and which stood in the centre of the grounds. The lower part of the house was fitted up and used as refreshment and tea rooms, and the upper portion retained as a residence for the Park-keeper until 1889, when it was demolished and the site cleared for the erection of a bandstand thereon. The Park-keeper is now located in a cottage near the Dudley Road entrance to the Park, also included in the original purchase. The Park is situated on the northwest side of the city, between the Dudley Road and Icknield Port Road, having entrances from both roads. The cost of laying out the grounds and erecting the two large entrance gates, with ornamental palisading the whole length of the Dudley Road frontage, was about £3,587, making a total expenditure of £11,587. Towards this amount a loan of £10,700 was obtained, repayable in sixty years. In 1883, Mr. Henry Weiss transferred to the Corporation a piece of land adjoining the Park, and containing a little over one acre in extent, subject to certain conditions, which included an additional entrance from the Gillott Road, and that other roads were formed at a cost of about £325.

At a meeting of the City Council, held on the 3rd of December, 1889, the Baths and Parks Committee reported that they had received an offer from Mr. William Morris, of Dudley Road, to sell five acres or thereabouts of his land

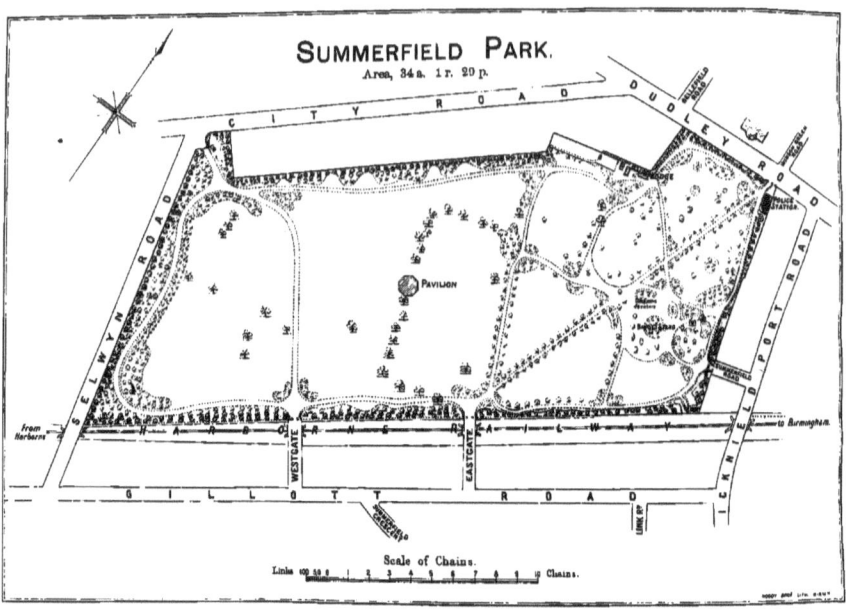

abutting on the western side of this Park, for the sum of £2,500. The Committee also reported that the City Surveyor had submitted to them a plan, prepared by Messrs. Chesshire, Gibson, and Co., showing the proposed laying out of the Rotton Park Estate preparatory to its being offered for sale, together with other information as to the formation of roads about to be constructed, subject to the necessary sanction of the Chancery Division of the High Court, to whom application was about to be made.

The Committee therefore pointed out to the Council that unless this land was acquired, no future extension of the Park would be possible, and as they had for a long time seen that its area, 13 acres, was altogether insufficient to meet the requirements of the large and increasing population of the neighbourhood, they had on several occasions approached Mr. Morris, in order to secure the land for its enlargement, but they had hitherto been unable to obtain from him a reasonable offer. The Committee therefore believed that the present opportunity should be taken advantage of, and recommended the Council to give the necessary authority to acquire the land in question for the sum of £2,500, and that the Finance Committee be instructed and authorised to borrow that sum under the provision of the statutes in that behalf.

It was moved by Mr. Alderman Barrow, seconded by Councillor Walsh, and

Resolved—

(15,192). That in accordance with the recommendations contained in the report of the Baths and Parks Committee now presented, the said Committee be and they are hereby authorised and instructed to purchase from Mr. William Morris about five acres of land, abutting on the western side of Summerfield Park, at a cost of £2,500, for the purpose of enlarging and improving the said Park; that the Finance Committee be instructed to borrow, under the provisions of the Statutes in that behalf, the sum of £2,500 for such purposes, and that for the several purposes aforesaid the said

Committees respectively do take all such steps, in the name and on behalf of this Council, and, when requisite, under the Corporate Common Seal, as they may deem advisable.

The sanction of the Local Government Board was subsequently obtained in respect thereto, and the work was carried out under the supervision of the City Surveyor and the officials of the Baths and Parks Department.

On the 6th of May, 1890, the Committee reported to the City Council that the conveyance from Mr. Morris to the Corporation of five acres or thereabouts of land adjoining Summerfield Park had been completed, and that with regard to the levelling, laying out, and planting of the land, the Committee estimated that the sum of £250 would be required for that purpose; also that it would be necessary to erect suitable fencing on the boundary adjoining the Gillott estate, at a cost of £300. The Committee further reported that they were unanimously in favour of the provision of a band-stand at this Park, as at present no accommodation existed for the shelter and protection of the band, as was the case at Victoria and Cannon Hill Parks. The Committee therefore proposed, with the sanction of the Council, to erect a suitable band-stand at a cost of £200.

The total sum proposed to be expended for the above-named purposes was £750, and by Resolution No. 15,315 the Committee were authorised to proceed with the several works at the cost named.

On the 5th day of May, 1891, the Baths and Parks Committee further reported to the City Council that they had had under consideration the probable erection of dwelling-houses on the north-west side of Summerfield Park, the only remaining direction in which any extension of the Park was possible, and stated that the Park is bounded on its other sides by the Dudley Road, the backs of houses abutting on the Icknield Port Road, and the Harborne Railway; and the land on the north-west side, which is the property of the trustees of the late Joseph Gillott, is now mapped out, and will shortly be offered for building purposes.

E

The Committee therefore found themselves confronted with the imperative necessity of taking steps to secure a portion of this land, or of abandoning any future hope of extending the boundaries of the Park, however desirable such extension may eventually appear.

The Committee also desired to point out to the Council that the Park is situated in a populous and rapidly developing district. Its present area is only 18a. 0r. 9p., and while on general grounds an addition to this area would be of material value on a favourable opportunity arising, the existing circumstances compel immediate action.

The Committee further reported that they had, in conference with the City Surveyor, approached Messrs. Cheshire, Gibson, and Co., the Surveyors to the Gillott Trustees, and obtained from them a provisional offer of 16a. 1r. 20p., or thereabouts, at the rate of £550 per acre, with the condition attached that the Corporation shall construct a road shown on the plan, and adopt the same as a public highway.

The construction of such a road, in the event of the land referred to being acquired, presents great advantages, as, with the exception of a limited frontage to Dudley Road, the only approaches to the Park consist of narrow entrances from Icknield Port Road and Gillott Road.

The Committee consider that the offer made is fair and reasonable, having regard to the price per yard at which similar land in the immediate neighbourhood is being let on building leases. Before, however, the arrangements can be carried out, it will be necessary for the trustees to obtain the approval of the Chancery Division of the High Court.

The Committee therefore recommended the Council to authorise them to acquire from the Gillott Trustees (subject to the approval of the Chancery Division of the High Court) the piece of land in question, adjoining Summerfield Park, on the north-west side, 16a. 1r. 20p. or thereabouts, in extent, for the purpose of enlarging and improving the Park ; and to arrange for the construction of the road referred to, and that the Finance Committee be instructed and authorised to borrow the amount required for such purposes.

The recommendations of the Committee, contained in the foregoing report, were, after a short discussion, approved by the City Council; and they were authorised to adopt such measures, in the name and on behalf of the Council, as they may deem necessary for carrying their recommendations into effect. The Finance Committee were also authorised and instructed to borrow the sum of £9,700 for the purposes named. The interest and sinking fund thereon is estimated at £375 per annum.

Following are the details of the approximate cost to lay out, level, and drain the new piece of land, also to provide the additional iron fencing that will be required for the extended boundary, with two new entrance gates, one leading from the City Road on the north side of the Park, and one leading from the Gillott Road, on the western side. It is also proposed to erect additional shelters and closet accommodation in connection therewith:

Fencing Park side of new road with unclimbable iron railings	£400
Entrance gates and piers at the junction of City Road and new road, and a new approach from Gillott road	350
Closets and Urinals	200
Shelter	400
Drives and walks	350
Drainage of walks and buildings	100
Trees, shrubs, and planting	500
Fencing for shrubberies	100
Re-erecting unclimbable fencing in new position; supervision of works, Surveyor's charges, and sundries	150
	£2,550

These extensions have enabled the Committee to considerably improve and increase the area of the ornamental portion of this Park, by transferring the site for all games, such as cricket, football, etc., to the newly acquired land in the rear, and to lay out the land hitherto used for such purposes, adjoining the Dudley Road, with flower beds, shrubberies, and lawn. The total area of the Park, when completed, will be 34 acres 1 rood 29 poles, of which about 10 acres are laid out with walks and garden, lawn for tennis, and bowling green, etc.

The staff consists of one resident Park-keeper and three assistants. The annual cost of maintenance is about £400 per annum, including £200 for wages, and £40 for rates and taxes. There are two greenhouses, with an area of 95 square yards, for propagating plants used in this Park.

Victoria Park.
Area, 43 a. 2 r. 22 p.

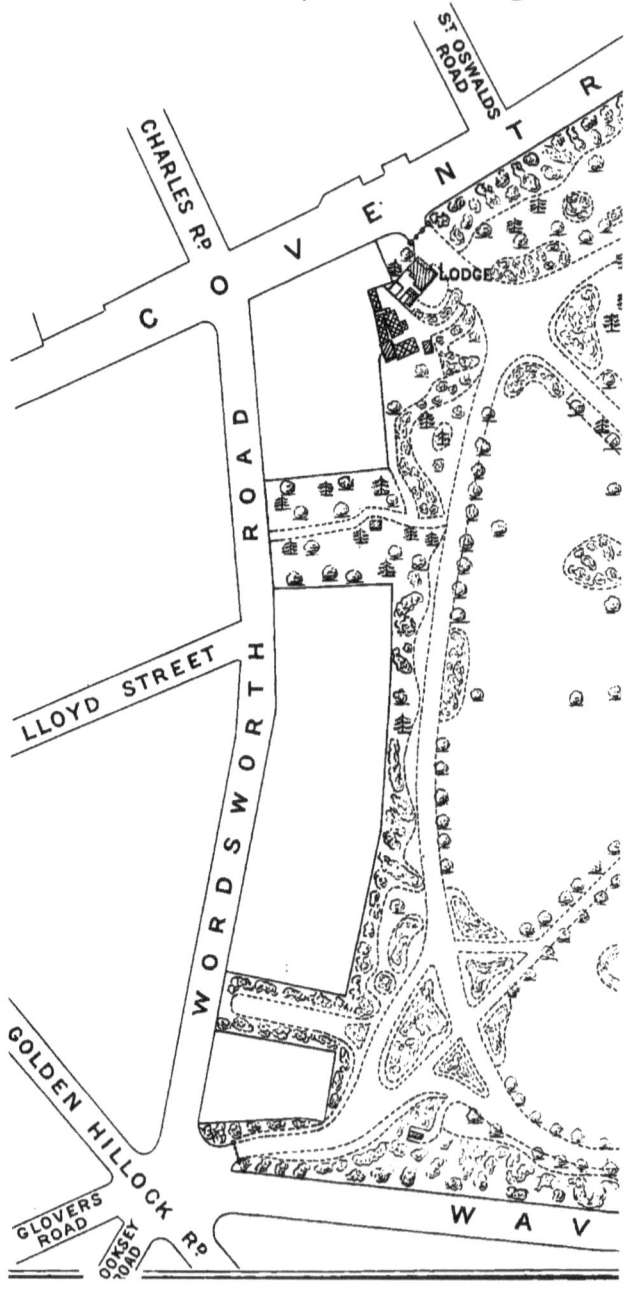

THE VICTORIA PARK, SMALL HEATH.

On the 2nd day of June, 1876, it was announced that Miss Ryland had offered another noble gift to the town, by the presentation of about forty-three acres of land in the Coventry Road, on the south-east side of the Borough, for the purpose of a Public Park for that district. At the time of its presentation, the land was in a state adapted for agricultural purposes, with the exception of that portion fronting Coventry Road, upon which stood the large mansion known as "The Rylands," and for many years the residence of General Dixon. This house was pulled down, and the site covered with lawn and shrubberies, etc., in 1883.

The estimates prepared by the Baths and Parks Committee for suitably converting the land for the purpose of a Park were deemed too costly by the Town Council, whereupon Miss Ryland, having approved of the plans, signified her wish to contribute £4,000 towards the outlay. With the aid of this contribution the Park was appropriately laid out by the Borough Surveyor, and a large pool constructed for boating and for the habitation of water fowl, and an ornamental refreshment room erected in the centre of the Park. This Park, like that at Cannon Hill, has the advantage of including a large number of old forest trees.

A large open-air swimming bath has also been formed, having a water area of 138 feet in length, with an average width of 70 feet, and fitted up with excellent dressing compartments and other conveniences.

The Park was opened to the public on the 5th day of April, 1879, during the mayoralty of Alderman Jesse Collings. The total cost of laying out, draining, and fencing in, with the

erection of the Park-keeper's lodge and the refreshment-room pavilion, and recent extensions, was about £16,000, reduced to £10,000 by Miss Ryland's two contributions of £4,000 and £2,000 respectively.

In the laying out of the Park, a piece of land containing about 3,250 square yards, having a frontage of 45 yards to the Wordsworth Road, was set apart as a possible site for the erection of a suite of Baths thereon. In 1880 a well was sunk on the site, at a cost of £1,300; and in 1887 the Baths and Parks Committee, with the approval of the Council, erected a new pumping station, with machinery in connection therewith, at a cost of £785, for the purpose of supplying the boating pool and the open-air swimming bath with water during the summer months. The total quantity of water required for this purpose during the season is about five million gallons.

A carriage drive, 24 feet in width, extends the whole distance round the Park. The land between this drive and the boundary fence on all sides is laid out with ornamental flower beds, shrubberies, and lawn, and the whole of the area within the drive is thrown open for the general use of the public, and upon which the various games of cricket, football, lawn tennis, &c., are played. The total area of the Park is 43½ acres, including about 27 acres of ornamental grounds and the various walks, which average from 9 to 16 feet in width.

In 1887, a band-stand, octagonal in shape, and constructed with iron columns and wood framework, was erected at the south-west side of the Park, at a cost of £150.

On the 23rd day of March, 1887, Her Majesty the Queen, accompanied by Their Royal Highnesses the Prince and Princess Henry of Battenberg, visited Birmingham; and shortly after their arrival at the Small Heath railway station, the Royal Party, accompanied by His Worship the Mayor, Alderman Thomas Martineau, Esq., and the Town Clerk, E. O. Smith, Esq., and escorted by a detachment of 7th Hussars, drove round the Park, entering and leaving through the principal entrance in Coventry Road. Previous to the arrival of the procession, from 40,000 to 50,000 school children had assembled, under the care of their respective teachers, for the purpose of giving Her Majesty a right royal welcome. The whole of the children were formed in two or three lines on each side of the carriage drive, the general public being excluded from the Park on that occasion.

To commemorate the event, Her Majesty subsequently gave permission, on the application of the Town Council through the Mayor, to substitute the name of "The Victoria Park" for that of Small Heath Park. The scene in the Park has also been selected as one of the subjects of the Jubilee memorial windows placed in the great hall of the Victoria Courts.

At a meeting of the Council on the 25th of October, 1887, the Committee reported that the land on the south and south-west sides of the Park was about to be appropriated for building purposes; and, with a view of preventing the erection of house property close up to the boundary of the Park, the Committee opened negotiations, through the Borough Surveyor, with Messrs. Willmott, Fowler, and Willmott, agents to the owner of the land, W. T. Taylor, Esq., and they ascertained that Mr. Taylor was willing to dispose of a strip of land on the two sides of the Park mentioned, and containing a total area of $1\frac{1}{4}$ acre, to the Corporation; Mr. Taylor was also willing to appropriate about 4 acres of the land adjoining for the purpose of forming a new roadway, 50 yards wide, providing the Corporation would erect suitable park fences for separating the Park from the new road, such fence to be of an ornamental character, and undertake to keep the said land so purchased open and used as a Park for ever. The Corporation were also to construct the new road, and sewer the same, Mr. Taylor to pay half the costs. The Surveyor estimated the cost to the Corporation as follows:

    Half-cost of Road   ... £1,800
    Cost of Park Railings   500
    Cost of $1\frac{1}{4}$ acre of Land   750
            ———
          £3,050

This amount was exclusive of labour for planting the new land, which, if done by workmen employed by the Committee, would not exceed £150. Miss Ryland having been informed of the proposals, most generously offered to present the sum of £2,000 towards the cost of the improvements, thus leaving the sum of £1,050 to be provided by the Corporation.

At a meeting of the Public Works Committee, on the 17th day of October, the Committee decided to relieve the Baths and Parks Committee of any further responsibility in respect to the formation of the new road; and, subject to the approval of the Council, to defray the cost out of the balance that Committee had received from the Drainage Board from tanks, etc., still in hand. The arrangement was approved by the Council by Minute No. 14,548, and on the motion of Mr. Alderman White, seconded by Mr. Alderman Barrow, the offer of Miss Ryland to contribute the sum of £2,000 was accepted, and the best thanks of the Council was given to that lady for her generous gift, and for another expression of her continued interest in the happiness and welfare of the inhabitants of the borough. The Baths and Parks Committee were thus enabled to improve the boundaries and plant shrubberies, and to erect strong wood fencing, running parallel with the new roads referred to. The Committee also removed the entrance gates from the Wordsworth Road to the junction of the Park with the Golden Hillock Road, Waverley Road, and Wordsworth Road, and they effected other improvements to the carriage drive leading therefrom, at an outlay of about £200.

There are four greenhouses erected at the rear of the Park-keeper's lodge, the whole having an area of 118 square yards; these are used for the cultivation of plants required in the Park. The staff consists of one resident Park-keeper and eight assistant gardeners.

The annual cost of maintenance is about £750, including £500 for wages, £22 rates and taxes, and £8 for tithe rent charge, &c.

There is an income of about £174 per annum derived from the following sources:

Letting of the Refreshment Room	...	£40	0	0
,,	Boating Pool ...	80	0	0
,,	Grazing Land	10	0	0
Incidentals from Games, &c. ...	...	44	0	0
Total	...	£174	0	0

BURBURY STRAND.

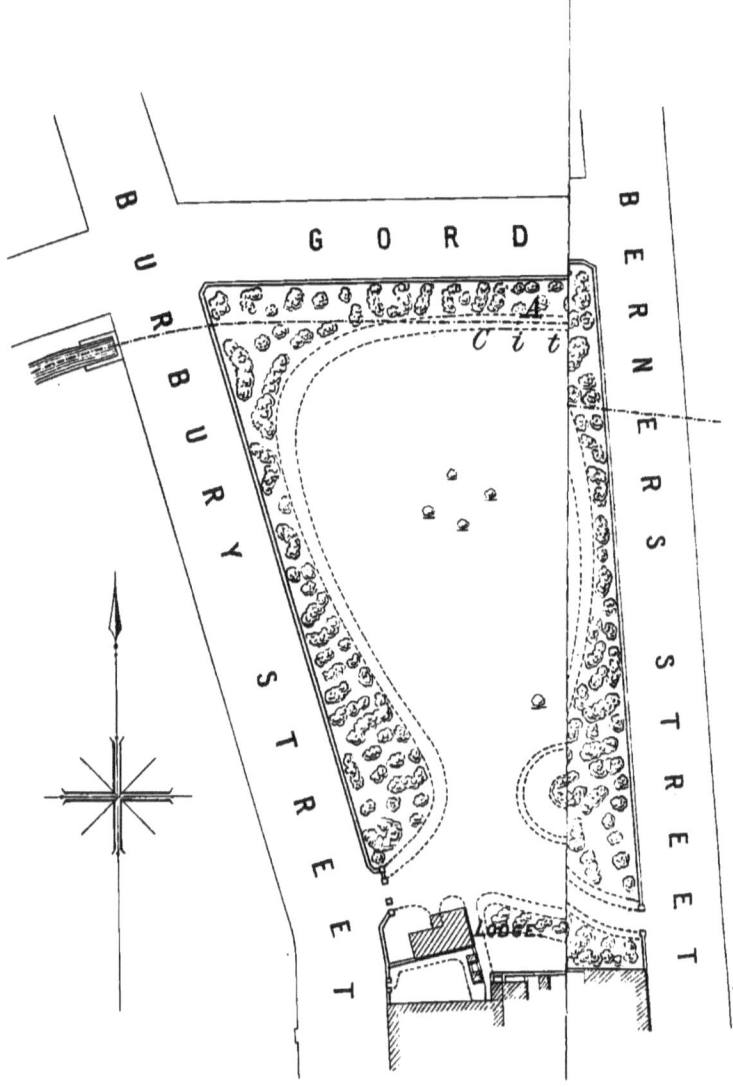

BURBURY STREET RECREATION GROUNDS,

Situated on the north side of the city, partly within and partly without the City boundary and the Manor of Aston. Its area consists of 4 acres 1 rood 3 perches, and is bounded on three sides by Burbury Street, Berners Street, and Gordon Street respectively, and on the fourth side by private property. The grounds are fenced in on the three sides named with dwarf brick walls and cast-iron ornamental palisading, with entrance gates from each street. The keeper's lodge is erected in conjunction with the principal entrance from Burbury Street. Nearly the whole of the ground is covered with asphalte, and serves as a valuable playground for that district. The borders on each side are laid out with ornamental flower beds and shrubberies, and in addition there are several large circular flower beds in the centre of the enclosure.

The land was presented to the Corporation by the late Mr. William Middlemore. The cost of laying out, fencing, and the erection of keeper's lodge was defrayed by that gentleman previous to the same being handed over to the Corporation.

The Grounds were formally opened to the public on the 1st day of December, 1877, by William Kenrick, Esq., Mayor.

The staff consists of one keeper, with an occasional assistant, and the annual cost of maintenance is about £250, including £65 for wages, £13 for rates and taxes, etc.

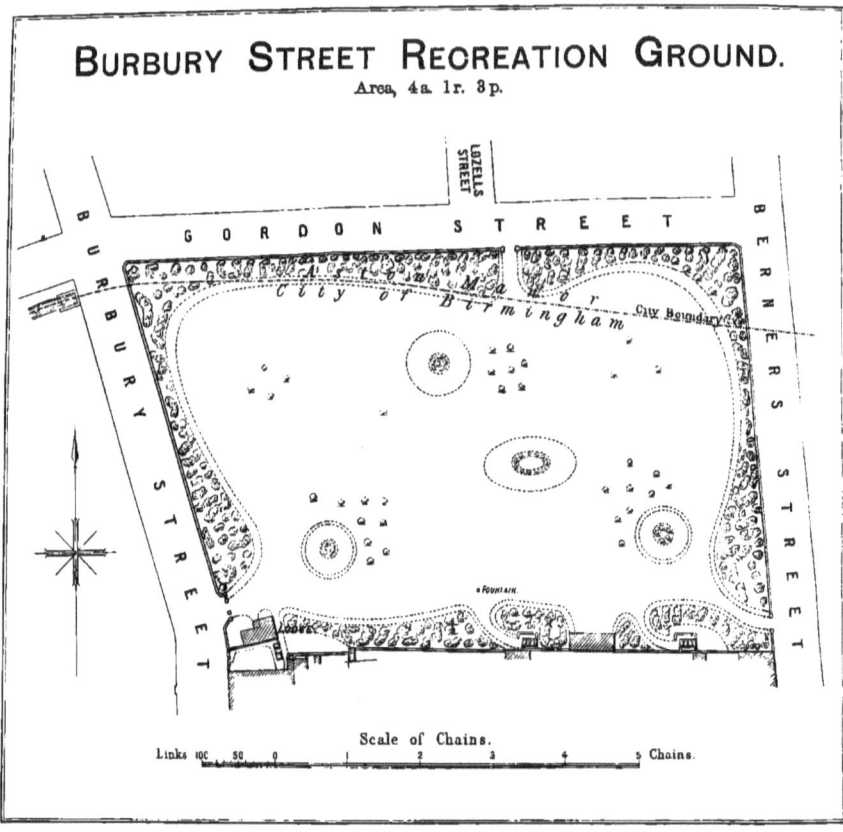

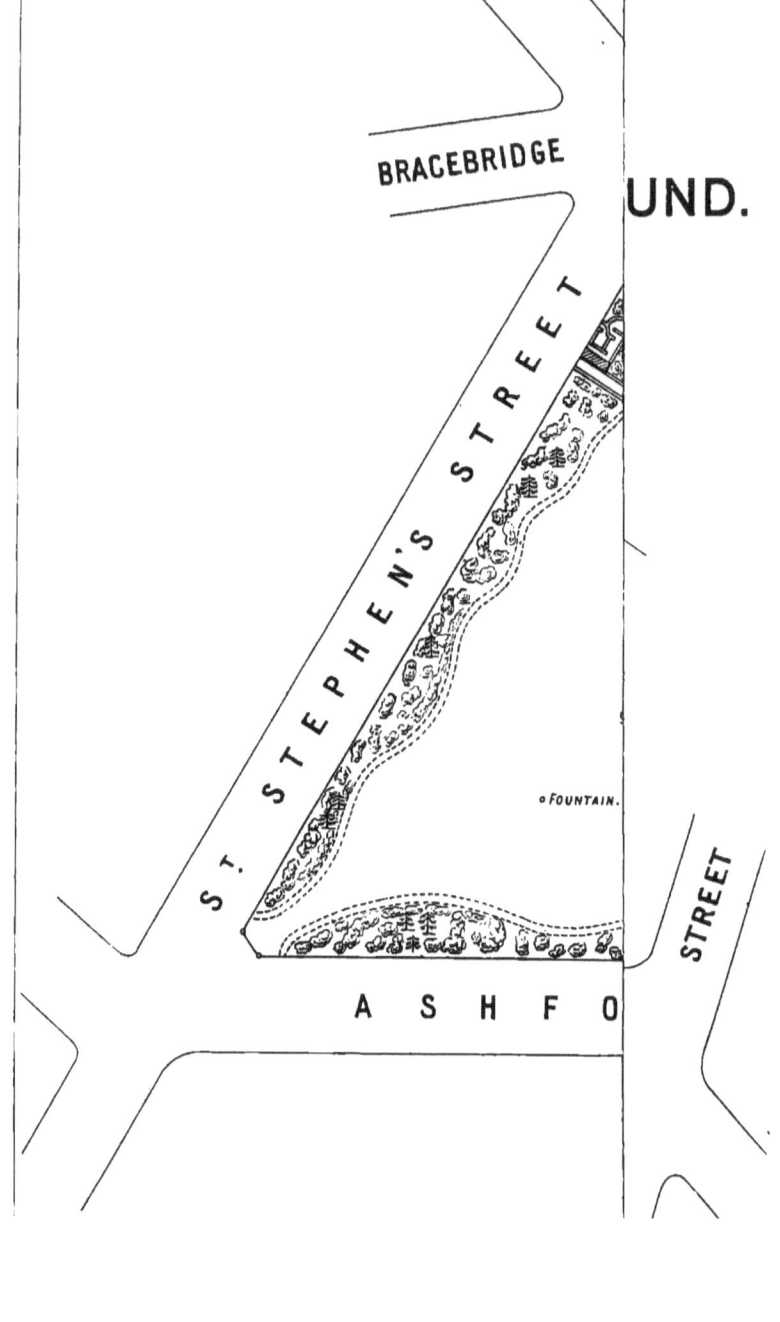

WALMER RECREATION GROUND.

At a meeting of the City Council, held on the 4th day of March, a memorial was presented by Mr. Councillor Pemberton from inhabitants, property owners, ratepayers, and manufacturers in the Northern district of Birmingham, praying that the piece of land, known as "The Old Pleck," situate between Newtown Row and Aston Road, might be obtained as a Recreation Ground for the use of the people. This memorial was referred to the Baths and Parks Committee for consideration, and to report thereon; and at a subsequent meeting of the Council, held on the 6th day of May, 1890, the Committee reported that they had made very careful and exhaustive inquiries on the subject, and that they had received and conferred with a deputation of gentlemen interested in the proposal.

The whole of the land comprises altogether about 23,383 square yards, or 4¾ acres, exclusive of St. Stephen's Street, which it was proposed to close if the whole scheme was carried out. The nearest Recreation Ground is about half a mile distant, viz., Burbury Street, and one mile from Aston Park. The land forms a portion of a large area laid out for building purposes, and is divided into two equal parts by St. Stephen's Street, and is offered on lease for that purpose.

The freehold is the property of the Governors of King Edward the Sixth's Grammar School, and was leased for 120 years, from Michaelmas, 1874, to Messrs. F. S. Bolton and the late Samuel Briggs, as representatives of the Midland Land Corporation, and subsequently re-assigned to these gentlemen absolutely.

The Committee having conferred with the City Surveyor, ascertained that the estimated cost of fencing in the Elkington Street, Ashford Street, and Bracebridge Street frontages with

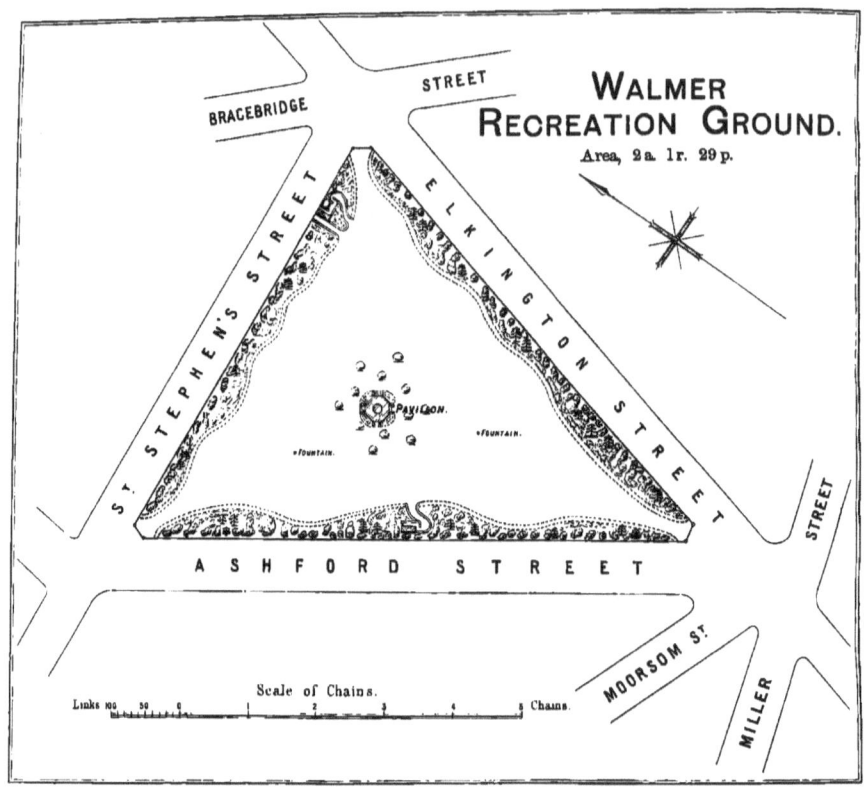

dwarf wall and iron palisadings, inclusive of entrance gates, would be £2,500; and if St. Stephen's Street was kept open throughout, the additional fencing would cost about £900 extra. Provision would also have to be made for paving in event of the street being closed.

The estimated cost to provide a lodge, shelter for children, closet accommodation, laying drains, regulating surface, etc., was set down at £2,000; and the cost of paving the remainder with limestone, £1,250, making a total cost of £5,750, and £6,650 if St. Stephen's Street remain.

The Committee further reported to the Council that the Governors of the Grammar School could not sell the freehold except with the consent of the Charity Commissioners, and that the Governors were unwilling to part with freehold land under any circumstances, although, in some instances, they have consented to exchange. If, however, the Council decided to lease the land, for the purpose of using it as a Recreation Ground, as they appear to have power to do under The Public Health Act, 1875, sec. 164, the terms upon which it might be secured are indicated in the following letter, written by Mr. Till (as trustee of the late Samuel Briggs) to His Worship the Mayor, on behalf of himself and Mr. F. S. Bolton:

"City of Birmingham,
"Surveyor's Department,
"The Council House,
"April 24th, 1890.
"Dear Mr. Mayor,
Since seeing you this morning, I have ascertained that Mr. F. S. Bolton would be willing to let on lease, for Recreation Ground purposes, the piece of land lying between Ashford Street, Elkington Street, and St. Stephen's Street, containing about 11,797 square yards; and the piece between St. Stephen's Street, Bracebridge Street, and Ashford Street, containing about 11,586 square yards, or either of them, at 5d. per square yard per annum. As surviving executor of the late Samuel Briggs, I concur in the proposition.

"Of course arrangements would have to be made with the freeholders (the Governors of King Edward's School) in respect of variation of the building covenants; but I do not anticipate there would be any difficulty as to this.

"Yours faithfully,
WILLIAM S. TILL.
" F. C. Clayton, Esq., J.P.,
" Mayor."

To the above rental of £487 per annum must be added the cost of maintenance and the repayment of the capital expenditure, the total of which is estimated at £1,000 per annum

For the purpose of testing the popularity of similar open spaces in the centre of the city, the Committee caused the persons passing through the undermentioned Recreation Grounds and Gardens, during the week ending 27th April, to be counted.

The return is as follows:

Day.	Date.	Burbury St. Recreation Ground.	Park Street Gardens.	St. Mary's Gardens.
Monday,	April 21	3,359	2,520	4,364
Tuesday,	,, 22	2,993	3,405	4,122
Wednesday,	,, 23	3,211	3,030	4,261
Thursday,	,, 24	3,055	2,980	4,660
Friday,	,, 25	3,321	3,604	5,055
Saturday,	,, 26	3,549	4,118	3,295
Sunday,	,, 27	4,039	5,246	2,795
		23,527	24,903	28,552

It must be borne in mind that the above are used as public thoroughfares, and that the numbers do not therefore accurately represent the persons using the grounds for recreation purposes. The Committee, therefore, having regard to the heavy cost incidental to the preservation of "The Old Pleck" as a Recreation Ground, reported that they were unable to agree on any recommendation to the Council thereon. The Council, after considerable discussion thereon, referred the report back to the Committee for further consideration.

At a meeting of the City Council, held on the 20th July, 1890, the Baths and Parks Committee submitted the following report upon the subject:

With regard to Minute of the Council No. 15,316, referring back to your Committee the consideration of the acquisition of "The Old Pleck" for a public Recreation Ground, your Committee now report that they have further considered the matter, as directed, and have held a special meeting, and, accompanied by His Worship the Mayor, visited the locality.

As will be remembered, the land comprises altogether about 4¾ acres, and is pretty equally divided by St. Stephen's Street into two triangular portions.

Your Committee cannot recommend the Council to take any steps to acquire the whole of "The Old Pleck"; but, having regard to the prayer of the memorialists, and the desirability of securing such an open space in a thickly populated neighbourhood, have considered the possibility of dealing with a portion thereof. The south portion, bounded by St. Stephen's Street, Ashford Street, and Elkington Street, and containing 11,586 square yards, appears the most suitable.

Your Committee have consulted with the city Surveyor, as to the reduction of the estimate for the fencing and laying out, etc., submitted to the Council on the 6th of May last, and are now of opinion that the erection of an unclimbable iron fencing may be substituted for a dwarf wall and palisading, and that a lodge may be dispensed with.

The Surveyor has accordingly prepared the following estimate for the half referred to, viz. :

Enclosing Land with Unclimbable Iron Fencing, 530 yards	£530
Regulating Surface	150
Limestone Paving, 10,000 square yards	850
Turf, Shrubs, Planting, Seats, etc.	150
Fencing Shrubberies	50
Erection of Closets, Urinals, and Drainage	150
Erection of Shelter	200
Sundries	20
	£2,100

The interest and sinking fund required to repay this amount, calculated on a thirty years' loan at 3¼ per cent., amounts to £109 per annum. The lease, which is the property of Mr. F. S. Bolton and the surviving executor of the late Mr. Samuel Briggs, is for a term of 99 years, and your Committee have reason to believe that the Governors of King Edward's School (the owners of the land) will be willing, subject to the approval of the Charity Commissioners, to waive the building covenants, and to accept the Corporation as lessees for the period named, at a rental of 5d. per square yard, which, calculated on 11,586 square yards (the total area of the piece in question), amounts to £241 7s. 6d. per annum, making a total annual charge of £350 7s. 6d.

Your Committee therefore recommend that they be authorised (subject to the approval of the Charity Commissioners) to take steps to acquire the portion of The Old Pleck referred to, on lease, from the Governors of King Edward's School, on the terms indicated; and that they be further authorised to fence and lay out the ground in the manner proposed in the report; and that they be authorised to take all such steps as may be requisite for the carrying out of the before-mentioned purposes, and, where necessary, under the Corporate Common Seal.

Your Committee also further recommend that the Finance Committee be instructed to borrow the sum required for the laying out of the land, viz., £2,100, under the provisions of the Statutes in that behalf.

It was moved by Mr. Alderman Barrow, seconded by Mr. Councillor Pemberton, and

Resolved—

(15,389) That, in accordance with the recommendation contained in the Report now presented, the Baths and Parks Committee be authorised to acquire a lease from the Governors of King Edward's School of the southern portion of the piece of land known as "The Old Pleck," bounded by St. Stephen's Street, Ashford Street, and Elkington Street, containing 11,586 square yards, for a term of 99 years, for the purposes of a public Recreation Ground, at a rental of £241 7s. 6d.

F

per annum; and to cause such ground to be properly fenced and laid out, at an estimated cost of £2,100. Also, that the Finance Committee be instructed to borrow, under the provisions of the Statutes in that behalf, the sum of £2,100; and that, for the purposes aforesaid, the said Committees respectively do take all such measures, in the name and on behalf of the Council, and, where necessary, under the Corporate Common Seal, as they may deem advisable.

The Local Government Board inquiry, in respect to the aforesaid loan, was held at the Council House on the 30th day of April, 1891, by John Thornhill Harrison, Esq., one of Her Majesty's Inspectors, acting for and under the authority of the said Board. The Chairman of the Baths and Parks Committee, Mr. Alderman Barrow, explained the details of the scheme, to which no opposition was offered; and subsequently the Town Clerk received the sanction of the Local Government Board thereto.

The lease was subsequently prepared by Messrs. Millward and Co., solicitors, of Waterloo Street, and sets forth that the area contains 11,586 square yards, leased for a period of ninety-nine years from the 25th March, 1891, at an annual rental of £245 14s. 7d.; and the various contracts have now been entered into for fencing in and laying out and paving the grounds, and for providing the necessary shelter and closet accommodation required in connection therewith.

The grounds are now planted with trees and shrubs adapted to the locality, and will be ready for opening to the public early in the year 1892, when the inhabitants of the district and others interested propose to celebrate the event by a public demonstration of some kind not yet determined upon.

The annual cost of maintenance, including interest and sinking fund, ground rent, and workmen's wages, etc., will amount to about £460 a year.

NECHELLS R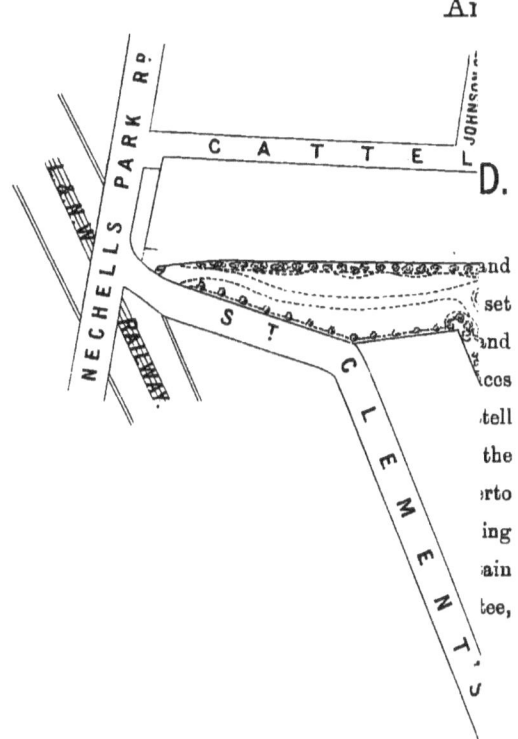

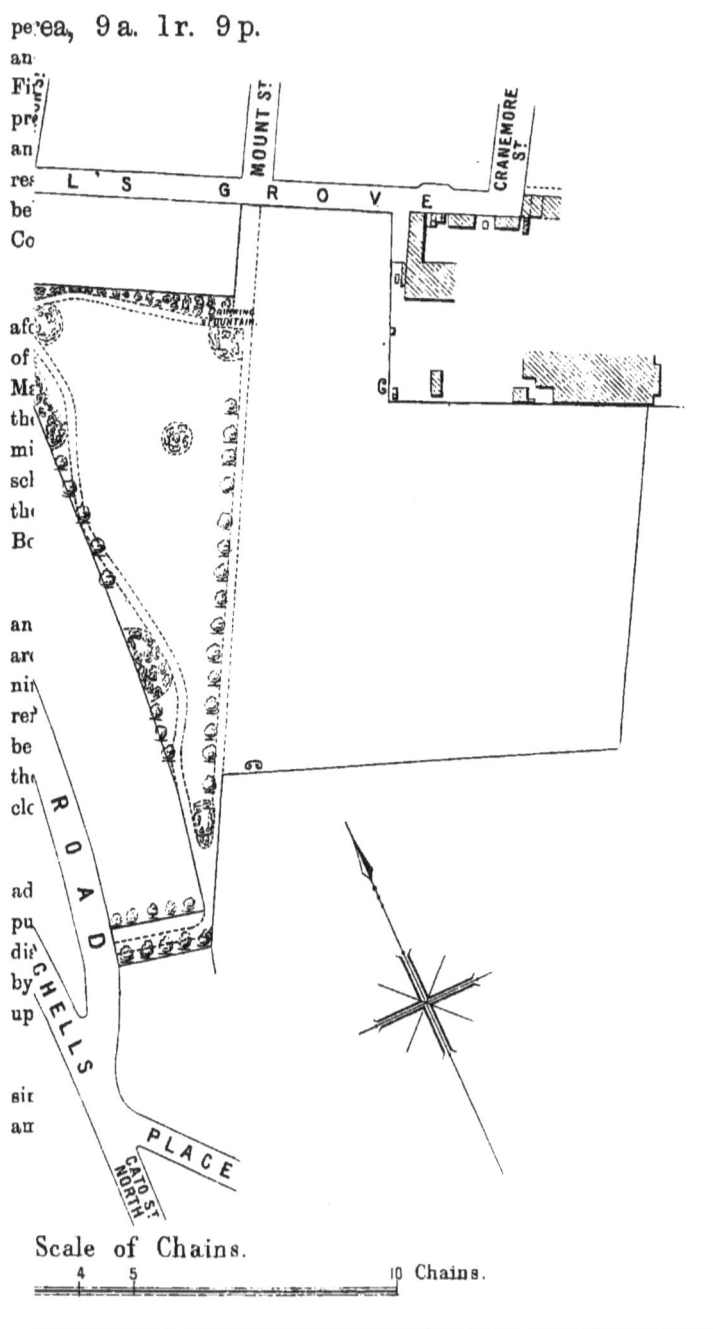

NECHELLS RECREATION GROUND.

The Gas Committee having acquired a large piece of land in this district for the extension of their works, they have set apart several acres as a Public Recreation Ground. The land has been laid out with turf and gravel walks, and has entrances from St. Clement's Road, Nechells Park Road, and Cattell Grove. The annual cost of maintenance is defrayed by the Gas Committee, under whose control the grounds have hitherto remained. The Baths and Parks Committee are now taking over the management of these grounds, subject to certain conditions contained in the offer made by the Gas Committee, and they hope to effect considerable improvements thereto.

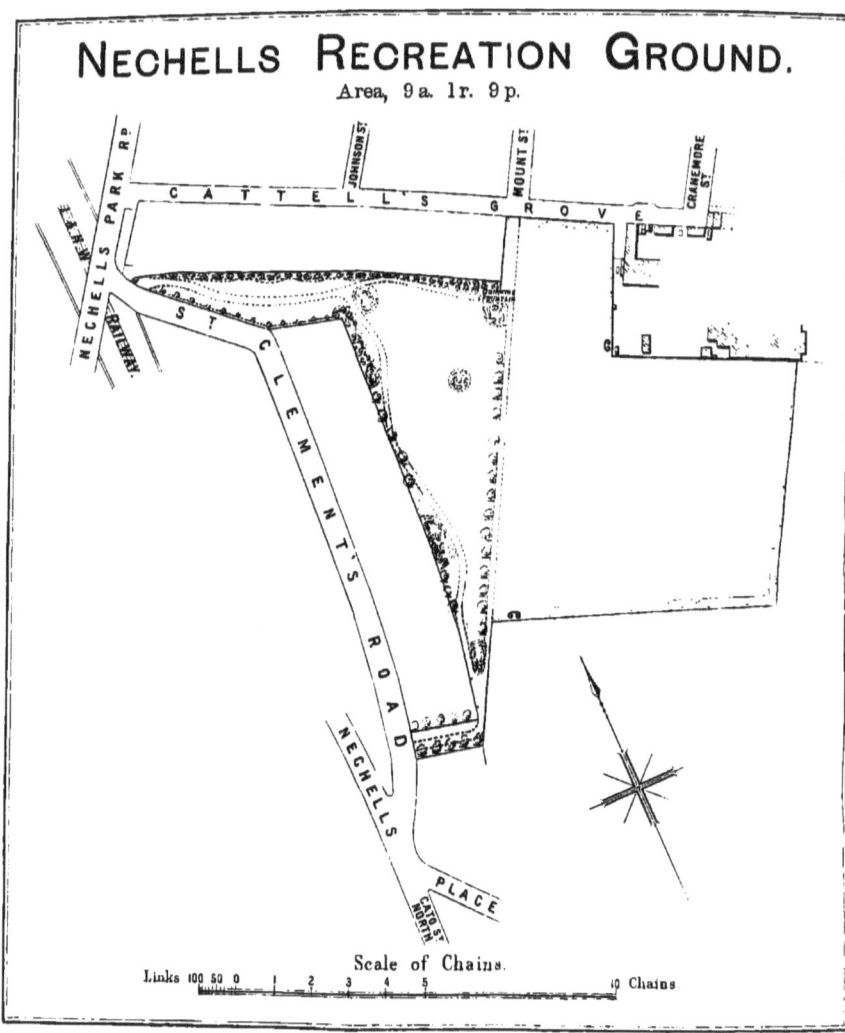

CLOSED BURIAL GROUNDS.

On the 12th of December, 1873, an Order in Council was issued by The Right Hon. Robert Lowe, Secretary of State, requiring—

(1) That no new burial ground be opened in the parishes of Birmingham, Edgbaston, and Aston.

(2) That burials be discontinued in St. John's Burial Ground, Liverpool Street; in the Jews' Burial Ground, Bartholomew Row and Granville Street; in the burial grounds of the Chapels in Cannon Street, Carrs Lane, Lombard Street, Newhall Street, Newtown Row, Graham Street, Bradford Street, and Steelhouse Lane; also in the churchyards of St. Philip's, St. Martin's, St. Bartholomew's, St. James's, St. Mary's, St. Paul's, St. Thomas's, St. George's, St. Peter's (Roman Catholic) Broad Street, and the Old Meeting House (now removed for the extension of the Central Railway Station), except in vaults and walled graves, with an air-tight coffin; also in the churchyards of St Matthew's, Holy Trinity, and Edgbaston Parish Church, except in existing family graves, and with coffins embedded in six inches of concrete.

Seeing that the churchyards no longer available for burials were, some of them, of an area sufficient to be valuable as playgrounds, and capable of being rendered ornamental, instead of disfigurements to the town, at the suggestion of Mr. C. E. Mathews, a member of the Estates Committee, the Corporation obtained in 1878 an Act giving them power, with the consent of The Bishop of Worcester and of the clergy of the respective parishes, to acquire possession of these spaces.

ST. MARY'S GARDENS.

At a meeting of the Council on the 5th April, 1881, a memorial was presented from the burgesses and inhabitants of St. Mary's Ward, praying the Council to take over the Graveyard attached to St. Mary's Church, and to maintain the same in decent order. The memorial was referred to the Estates Committee.

In 1882 considerable alterations and improvements in connection with this Churchyard were undertaken. The work of converting the whole of the area into a garden and playground was executed, from plans prepared by the City Surveyor, at a cost of £1,856, and for which a loan was effected. The total area, exclusive of the Church, is about 13,439 square yards (nearly three acres). About 5,970 square yards have been covered with asphalte, and a shelter provided; two new entrance gates, with massive brick and stone piers, have also been erected, one in Weaman Row and one in St. Mary's Row. Other improvements have been carried out in connection with the iron palisading with which the grounds are surrounded. These Gardens were formally opened on the 16th day of October, 1882, by Thomas Avery, Esq., Mayor, and the annual cost of maintenance is about £120.

PARK STREET GARDENS.

Under the powers of the Act mentioned, the Corporation, in 1879, took possession of the long-disused St. Martin's Burial Ground in Park Street, and of St. Bartholomew's Churchyard, an area, altogether, of about five acres, and converted them into Public Recreation Grounds, which were to be known as Park Street Gardens.

The work, together with that of improving the old burying ground of St. Martin's, adjoining the Church, was executed at a cost of £10,263. Of the area mentioned, half an acre was thrown into the adjoining streets, the widening of which constituted a great improvement; and of the amount

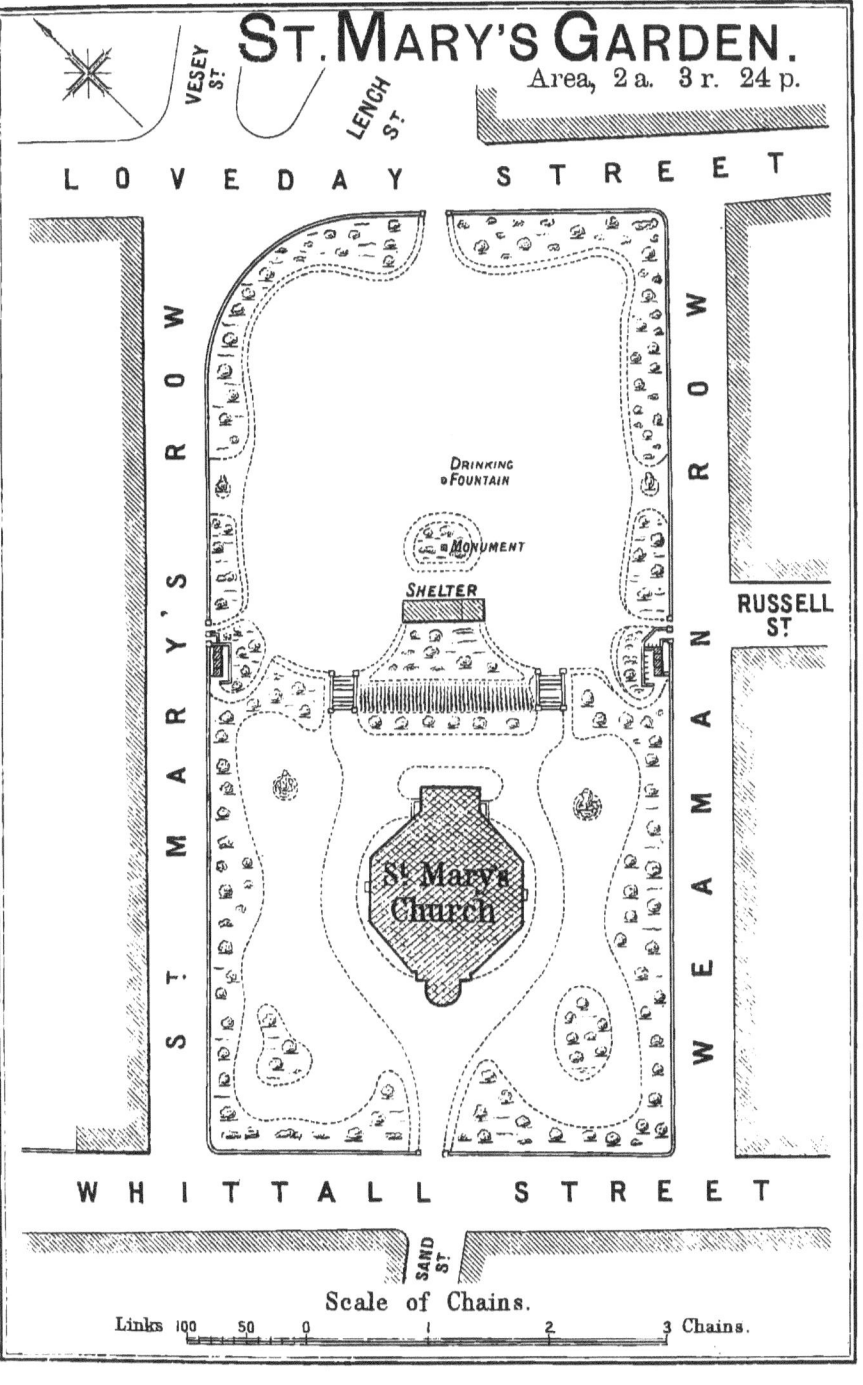

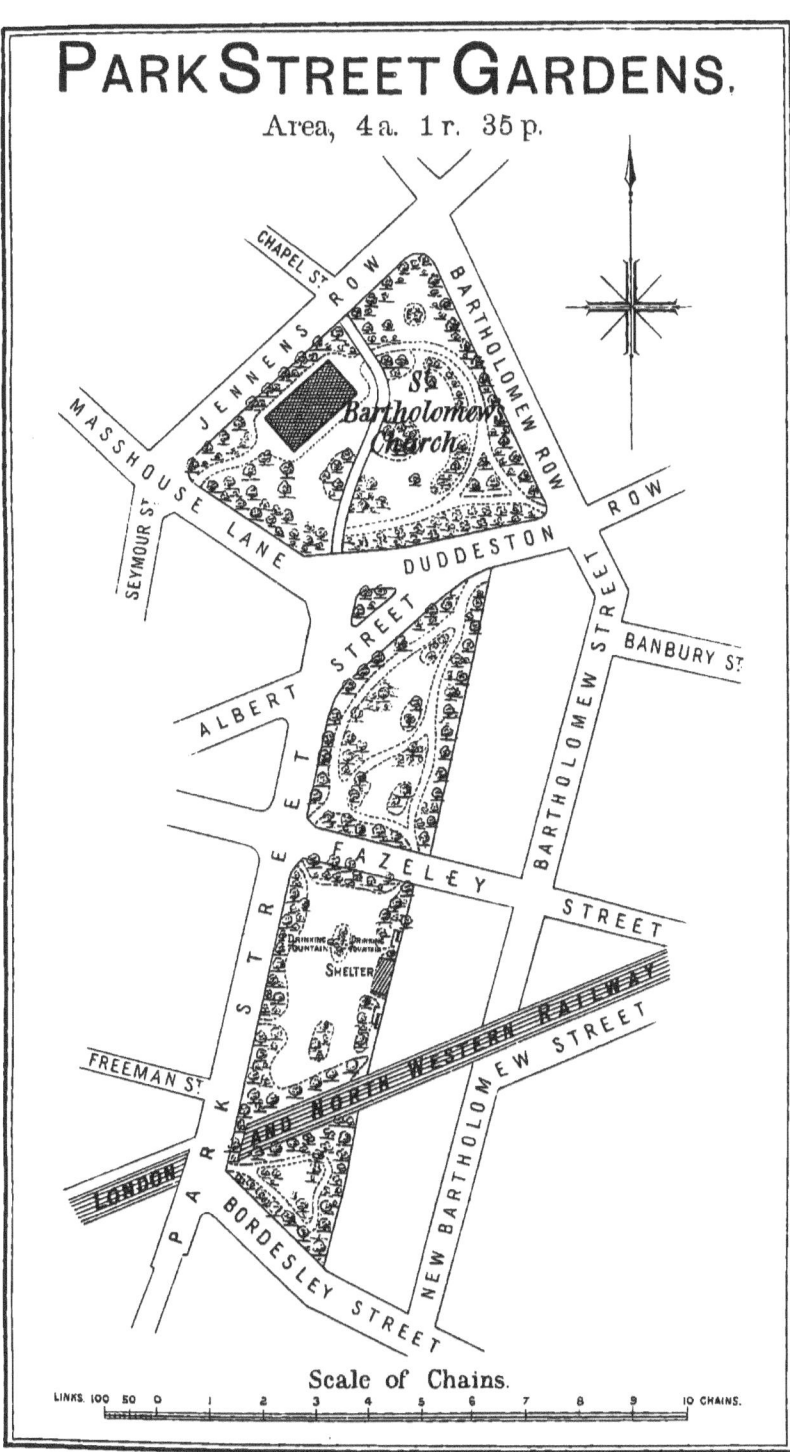

named, £2,943 was paid by the Public Works Committee, as an apportionment of public street improvements in connection therewith.

The area of the Gardens, about four acres and a half, is planted with trees and shrubs, and interspersed with flower beds, etc. A portion of the area is asphalted, to serve as a playground for children, and suitable shelters have been erected, with other accommodation for the comfort and convenience of visitors thereto.

The grounds were opened by the Mayor, Mr. Alderman Richard Chamberlain, on the 25th of June, 1880. The annual cost of maintenance is about £300. Nearly the whole of the area is enclosed with a low brick wall and cast-iron palisading, with entrance gates from each of the streets abutting thereon.

For the capital expenditure, a loan, repayable in sixty years, was raised.

ST. MARTIN'S CHURCHYARD.

This Churchyard has been greatly improved by the Corporation, and part of the site was taken from it to widen the adjacent streets. The work was executed in 1880, the outlay being included in the loan raised for the Park Street Gardens. The planting and renewal of trees, turf, etc., and the general maintenance of the iron palisading surrounding the Churchyard, is carried out at the cost of the Corporation.

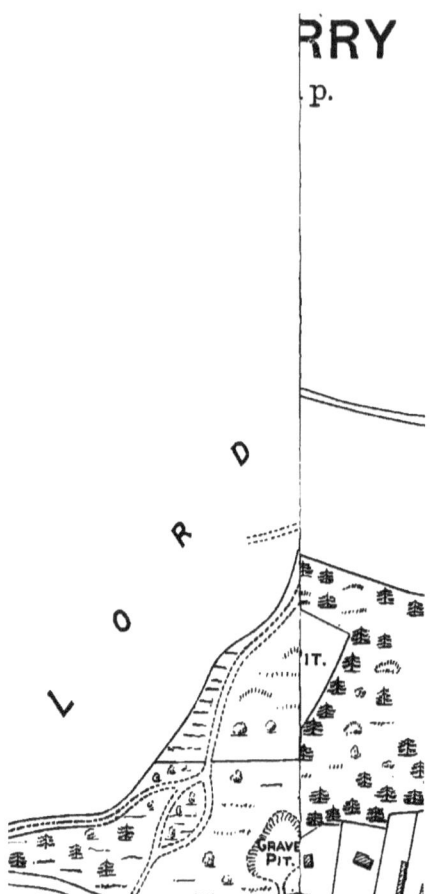

REDNAL AND BILBERRY HILLS

Are situated on the direct Bristol Road between Birmingham and Bromsgrove, about nine miles from the former and six miles from the latter. The nearest railway station is Barnt Green, on the Midland Railway, and is about one and a half mile distant. There is also a station at Rubery, on the Great Western Line, about the same distance on the northern side of the Hill. They form part of a range known as the Bromsgrove Lickey Hills, Rednal Hill being on one side of the main road and Bilberry Hill on the other side. The latter derives its name from the large number of bilberry bushes growing thereon. Both Hills are well wooded, and from each extensive and beautiful views are obtained of the surrounding country.

At a meeting of the Council, held on the 28th day of December, 1887, the Mayor, Sir Thomas Martineau, read two letters he had received, one from Mr. T. Grosvenor Lee, and one from Lord Windsor, in reply to inquiries which had been made as to the progress of a scheme for the acquisition of Rednal Hill for public purposes.

Mr. Lee in his reply, dated December 12th, 1887, reported that on the 11th of October he had agreed to purchase from Messrs. A. E. Wenham, R. H. Millward, and T. B. Osborne, at the price of £1,000, about 22 acres of uncultivated land on Rednal Hill, and which had been advertised to be sold by public auction, in small building lots, on the evening of that day. Mr. Lee further stated, his object in making the purchase was to endeavour to secure the purchase and preservation of the greater part of the Hill, in its present striking, wild, and picturesque condition, for the enjoyment of the public for ever. Since the date of the above-mentioned purchase, Mr. Lee reported that he had succeeded in buying back again from the various owners a considerable part of the northern portion of the Hill, which had been sold in lots at a previous auction in

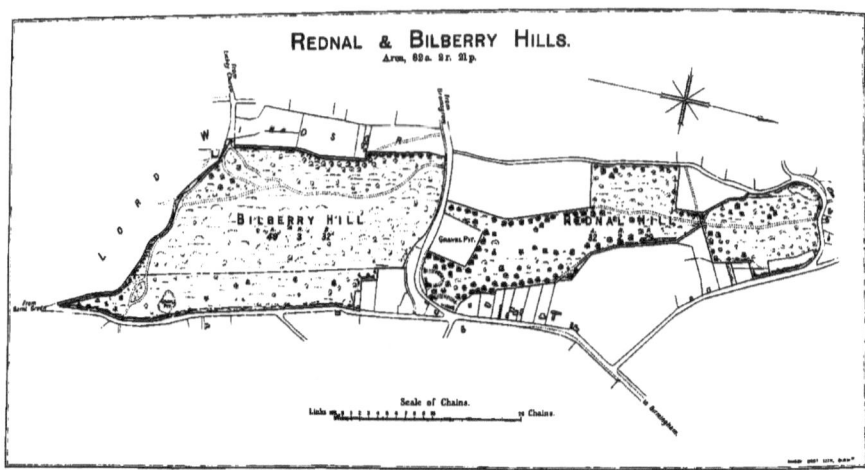

August last; and consequently Mr. Y.Underhill, of Small Heath, who had offered to present to the public the uncultivated portion of the lots purchased by him if the other lots could be acquired, was then prepared to carry out the previous intention, which he then expressed : " The land recently acquired, added to the 22 acres previously purchased by me, made a total of 30 acres, purchased at a total cost of £1,500, and it is possible that an additional four acres may be eventually acquired. It must, however, be remembered that the land, although secured, is not yet paid for, and the possibility of carrying out the whole scheme must depend upon the way in which the public respond to the appeal for subscriptions which will be issued early in the ensuing year, it having been considered undesirable to issue such appeal during the progress of the negotiations which have recently been going on. Several promises of pecuniary support have already been received, and if a sufficient sum is raised to enable me to purchase the whole of the 30 acres, next March it is proposed (subject of course to the approval of those who subscribed the purchase money) that the Hill should be transferred to the Corporation of Birmingham, or some other responsible public body willing to undertake the charge of it, subject only to a condition that it shall be kept open for ever for the enjoyment of the public.
" (Signed)
" T. GROSVENOR LEE,
" *Hon. Sec. of the Birmingham Association for the Preservation of Open Spaces and Public Footpaths.*"

Lord Windsor's letter upon the same subject, dated from Hewell Grange, Bromsgrove, December 5th, 1889, is as follows:

" Dear Sir Thomas Martineau,

" With reference to the conversation which we had last month at the Conservative Club in Birmingham, I wish to say that I am prepared to grant a lease of Bilberry Hill, for purpose of recreation, for 21 years (reserving, however, a width of ground fronting the main road), at an annual rental of £5, towards the payment of which I will subscribe £5 per annum.

" A plan will be prepared, and all necessary particulars arranged, by my Agent, to whom I have given instructions to carry out the details.
" (Signed) WINDSOR."

These letters were received by the Council, and referred to the Baths and Parks Committee by Minute No. 14,626, with instructions to consider the proposals therein respectively contained, and to make the necessary inquiries in reference thereto, and to report to the Council thereon. A cordial vote of thanks was also presented by the Council to Lord Windsor for the generous offer contained in his letter.

On the 1st of May, 1888, the Baths and Parks Committee reported to the Council that they had visited Rednal and Bilberry Hills, and they believed that the offers made by Lord Windsor, Mr. Grosvenor Lee, and the subscribers, will result in a valuable addition to the Recreation Grounds now under the control of the Council, and they recommended that the offers be accepted.

At the same meeting of the Council, the Mayor (Mr. Alderman Pollack) read a letter from Mr. Grosvenor Lee, stating that the amount raised by public subscription—which was opened by the Association of which he was the Hon. Secretary (viz., The Birmingham Association for the Preservation of Open Spaces and Public Footpaths)—had been sufficient to enable them to complete the purchase of the southern portion of Rednal Hill, comprising 21 acres, and that the contributors to the fund were willing that the portion so purchased should be transferred as a free gift to the Corporation of Birmingham, if they are willing to take the charge of it, with the object of its being kept open for ever as a place of public recreation and enjoyment.

Mr. Lee suggested that if the gift was accepted, some person should at once be appointed to take charge of the Hill, as well as the Bilberry Hill presented by Lord Windsor. Mr. Lee also stated that the money raised up to that date, May 1st, 1888, was about £500 less than the amount required for purchasing the northern portion of the Hill, about $7\frac{1}{2}$ acres, and for securing the free gift of $1\frac{1}{2}$ acre in addition, kindly offered by Mr. Underhill on condition that the $7\frac{1}{2}$ acres were acquired. Mr. Lee further reported that he had arranged with the vendors for an extension until the 4th of August next, the time within which it must be decided whether the latter portion of the Hill is to become the property of the public, or is to be cut up into eight building plots, into which it has already been divided on paper; and Mr. Lee wrote: "I trust that when the public attention is directed to the great importance of securing the whole of the Hill, for the purpose of preserving it in its present wild and picturesque condition, for ever, the necessary funds will be forthcoming during the next three months."

By Minute No. 14,766, the Council accepted the generous offer made by The Right Hon. Lord Windsor, to grant a lease of Bilberry Hill for 21 years, at a rental of £5 per annum, subject to the condition contained in his lordship's letter of December 5th, 1887; and by the same minute the Baths and Parks Committee were instructed, on the completion of the lease, to receive possession of the ground, and to take all measures, as they may deem necessary, for the preservation and maintenance of the same as a place for public recreation; and, further, that the Town Clerk be instructed to affix the Corporate Common Seal to all deeds, instruments, and writings necessary for giving effect to the resolution.

By Minute 14,767, the Council resolved to accept the offer made by Mr. T. Grosvenor Lee, to transfer to the Council 21¼ acres of land, forming a part of the Rednal Hill, as a free gift to the Corporation, subject to the condition that it shall be kept open for use as a place of recreation and enjoyment for the public. The Baths and Parks Committee were also instructed to receive possession of the land on the completion of the transfer, and to take all such measures as they may deem necessary for the preservation and maintenance thereof, as a place of public recreation, at the cost of the borough; and, further, the Town Clerk was instructed to affix the Corporate Common Seal to all deeds, instruments, and writings necessary for giving effect to the resolution.

The Hills were declared open to the public on the 19th day of May, 1888, by Sir Thomas Martineau, Mayor; the members of the Baths and Parks Committee, with other members of the Council, and the officials of the department, being present. The annual cost of maintenance is about £70, including wages, rates, and taxes.

On the 2nd day of July, 1889, the Baths and Parks Committee reported to the Council that the lease from Lord Windsor, of Bilberry Hill, had been sealed and exchanged; and with regard to the Rednal Hill, the Committee reported Mr. Grosvenor Lee had lodged the title deeds of the major portion of the property with the Town Clerk, with an undertaking to convey the whole to the Corporation when the purchases yet to be made had been effected.

At the same meeting of the Council, the Committee reported that large numbers of persons visited the Hills, especially on Bank Holidays, and that, although it was the practice to send two additional men for special duty on such days, they proposed to communicate with the county authorities, and urge that some assistance should be afforded the local police officers at all times when large numbers of persons were expected to visit the locality. This application met with the ready response of the Authorities, and eight constables, with two sergeants, are now placed on duty in the neighbourhood upon all such occasions.

At a meeting of the City Council, held on the 3rd day of December, 1888, the Mayor read the following letter from Mr. T. Grosvenor Lee:

"18, Newhall Street,
"Birmingham,
"11th November, 1889.
"To His Worship the Mayor of Birmingham.
"Dear Sir,
"Referring to the communications which have passed between The Open Spaces Preservation Association and your two immediate predecessors, on the subject of Rednal Hill, I have now the great satisfaction of informing you that the whole money required for completing the purchase of the northern portion of Rednal Hill (about seven hundred pounds) has been raised by public subscription ; and I am now prepared to convey that portion of the Hill, containing an area of about nine acres, to the Corporation of Birmingham as a free gift, subject only to the condition that it shall be kept open for ever as a place for public recreation and enjoyment. Mr. George

Underhill has honourably fulfilled the pledge which he gave in August, 1887, by making a free gift to the Corporation of two plots of land on the Hill, containing about one and a half acre, which he purchased at the first auction. The Committee who have had charge of the matter regret, however, to report that the owners of two plots on the Hill have hitherto absolutely declined to sell their land for the purpose of making the scheme complete, and the existence of these plots in private hands must always be to some extent a public injury. It is hoped that at some future time the proprietors will be willing to follow the excellent example set to them by the other owners of separate lots, and will consent to sell their land to the Corporation at a fair price.

"I remain, Sir,
"Yours obediently,
"T. GROSVENOR LEE,
"Hon. Sec. of above Association."

It was moved by the Mayor, seconded by Alderman Sir Thomas Martineau, and
Resolved—

(15,165) That Mr. Grosvenor Lee's letter be received, and referred to the Town Clerk, with authority to accept a conveyance to the Corporation of the land described therein, forming the northern portion of Rednal Hill, and to take all such measures as may be necessary for completing the transfer of such land, on the conditions and in accordance with the directions contained in Council Minute No. 14,767, of the 1st of May, 1888, and that the completion of the transfer be notified to the Baths and Parks Committee.

It was moved by the Mayor, seconded by Alderman Sir Thomas Martineau, and
Resolved—

(15,166) That the best thanks of this Council be presented to Mr. George Underhill, for his free gift to the Corporation of two plots of land on Rednal Hill; and to Mr. T. Grosvenor Lee, for his indefatigable and disinterested exertions in promoting and carrying out the scheme by which the Corporation have become possessed of this valuable property, for the use and enjoyment of the inhabitants of this city and the neighbourhood for ever.

STREET ENCLOSURES.

There are numerous places in the city where plantations have been made in the open spaces at the convergence of several streets. The largest is in Summer Hill Terrace, and affords a good example of this kind of street ornamentation. There are other enclosures at the junctions of the following streets, the whole of which are enclosed with ornamental palisading:

      Buckingham Street with Hampton Street.
      Lawley Street   ,,   Great Barr Street.
      Anderton Road   ,,   Grantham Road.
      Gosta Green.
      Camden Square.

Flowers and ornamental shrubs are also placed on the Sturge memorial at the Five Ways, on the Attwood statue in Stephenson Place, and in the ornamental spaces adjoining the Town Hall and Council House.

A Plantation was maintained for several years on the grounds of the Water Committee at Whitacre, and was used principally as a nursery for growing shrubs and trees required in the roads and street enclosures, etc. This land was given up to the Water Committee in June, 1891, as the Baths and Parks Committee found they had enough spare land at the various Parks suited for that purpose.

TREES IN STREETS.

The care and maintenance of the trees planted in some of the principal streets and roads of the city was formerly under the Public Works Committee. On the 2nd of January, 1883, the Public Works Committee recommended the Council to transfer the management thereof to the Baths and Parks Committee. The necessary openings in the footpaths for the planting of fresh trees, and the making good of the pavement after renewals, &c., were to be carried out by the Public Works Committee as heretofore. The recommendation was approved by the Council by Minute No. 12,995. The annual cost of such maintenance and renewals, etc., is about £60.

TREES ARE PLANTED IN THE UNDERMENTIONED STREETS AND ROADS OF THE CITY, AS FOLLOWS—

Situation.	Birch.	Chestnut.	Elm.	Lime.	Plane.	Poplar.	Total.
Aberdeen Street	...	...	...	...	2	...	2
Bristol Road	...	...	...	328	5	...	333
Bristol Street	...	...	...	66	4	6	76
Broad Street	...	...	...	...	63	...	63
Berner Street	...	...	...	...	8	...	2	10
Buckingham Street	...	...	...	6	...	...	6
Burbury Street	...	...	...	...	9	...	2	11
Chamberlain Memorial	...	...	...	...	4	...	4
Congreve Street	...	...	...	...	...	1	...	1
Camp Hill	...	...	...	2	5	...	7
Dudley Road	...	...	...	...	1	...	1
Edmund Street	...	...	...	...	3	...	3
Edgbaston Road	...	...	...	9	...	...	9
Grantham Road	...	...	...	...	34	...	34
Gosta Green	...	...	...	...	...	4	4
Gough Road	...	...	...	...	16	...	16
Icknield Street	...	...	...	8	...	...	8
James Watt Street	...	...	...	...	5	...	5
Lower Temple Street	...	...	...	...	...	1	1
Moseley Road	...	...	...	2	15	...	17
Nechells Place	...	...	...	...	4	2	6
Nechells Park Road	...	...	...	53	18	7	78
Pershore Road	...	...	...	148	20	...	168
Summerfield Road	...	...	...	6	...	...	6
Stanmore Road	4	...	...	12	...	...	16
Stephenson Place	...	...	...	...	7	10	17
Stephenson Street	...	...	...	...	1	...	1
Sir Harry's Road	...	...	...	...	4	...	4
Speedwell Road	...	...	...	...	5	...	5
Sandy Lane	...	...	1	...	...	...	1
Sandpits	...	...	...	...	12	...	12
Watery Lane	...	...	...	...	...	6	6
Wheeleys Road	...	...	1	...	59	...	60
	4	1	15	652	279	40	991

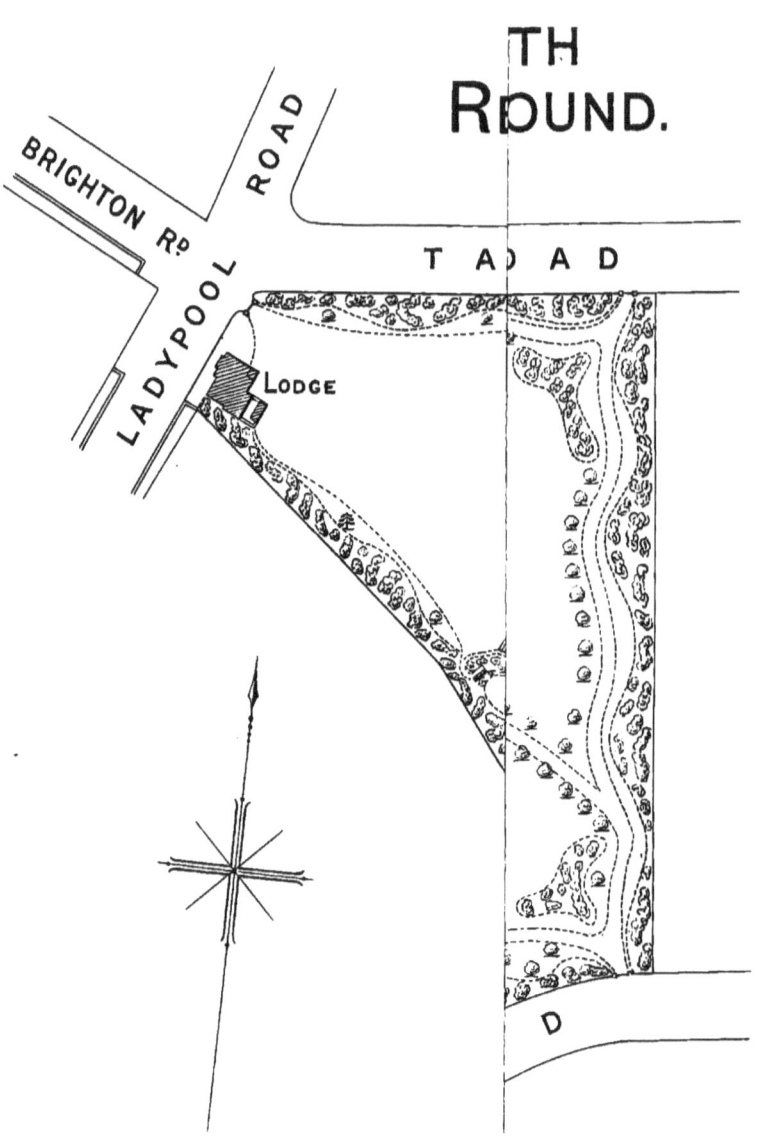

BALSALL HEATH RECREATION GROUND.

Previous to the annexation of Balsall Heath to the City, the Local Board of that district undertook to acquire from W. C. A. Smith-Ryland, Esq., a piece of land in Ladypool Lane, Sparkbrook, containing about $4\frac{1}{2}$ acres, for the purpose of a Recreation Ground, on lease for a term of twenty-one years, at an annual nominal rent, which will be paid by Mr. Smith-Ryland. The Local Government Board also sanctioned a loan of £3,500 for the erection of a keeper's lodge, fencing in, and laying-out of the grounds.

By the City of Birmingham Order, 1891, and the Act confirming the same, this piece of land was taken over by the City Council, and placed in charge of the Baths and Parks Committee, as and from the 9th of November, 1891.

On the 5th day of January, 1892, the Committee reported to the City Council that the boundaries of the land in question had not yet been settled, and that when such settlement had been arrived at, the lease would be signed by the Corporation.

At the same meeting of the Council, the Finance Committee were authorised and instructed to borrow the sum of £3,500, for the purpose of laying out the grounds, etc., in accordance with the arrangements previously made by the Balsall Heath Local Board.

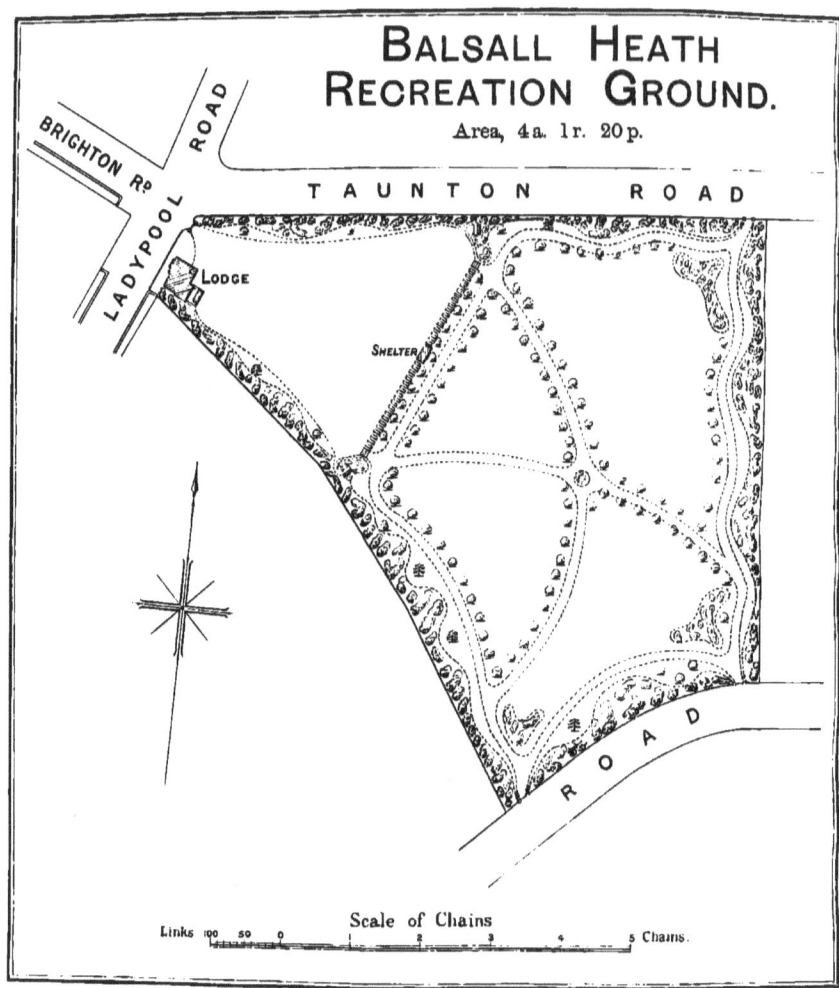

DETAILED STATEMENT OF THE ANNUAL INCOME DERIVED FROM THE SEVERAL PARKS AND GARDENS, FOR THE YEAR ENDING MARCH 31, 1891.

NAME OF PARK.	Rent of Refreshment Rooms.			Rent of Boating Pools.			Rent of Swimming Bath.			Rent of Grazing Land.			Income from Cricket.			Income from Football.			Income from Lawn Tennis.			Income from Bowls.			Income from Croquet.			Income from Hire of Chairs.			Income from Sale of Grass.			Miscellaneous Income.			Total Amount of Income. 1891.		
	£	s.	d.	£	s.	d.	£	s.	d.	£	s.	d.	£	s.	d.	£	s.	d.	£	s.	d.	£	s.	d.	£	s.	d.	£	s.	d.	£	s.	d.	£	s.	d.	£	s.	d.
Aston Park	40	0	0										8	15	0	3	19	6	1	10	0	10	10	3				1	4	10		7		0	10	0	68	4	9
Cannon Hill Park	40	0	0	120	0	0	40	0	0	35	0	0	0	25	7	3	2	6	0	22	3	0	13	6	3	0	0	2	3	3	3	9		6	13		4 329	12	0
Victoria Park	60	0	0	80	0	0				10	0	0	0	13	1	0	4	15	0	18	1	0	6	6										6	2	10	5 174	7	0
Calthorpe Park	40	0	0							20	0	0	0	21	19	0	3	10																			55	9	0
Alderley Park	10	0	0							5	0	0	0	5	0	0	1	16																			11	16	0
Burbury Street Recreation Ground																																							
Highgate Park																															0	14	0	0	12	6	1	6	6
Summerfield Park																			3	7	4	1	10	9							3	12	3	2	11	0	11	1	4
Park Street Gardens																																							
St. Mary's Gardens																																							
Street Enclosures																																							
Trees in Streets																																							
Rednal Hills										1	4	0																			0	7	6				1	11	6
Totals	150	0	0	200	0	0	10	0	0	71	4	0	74	3	0	17	2	0	45	2	0	13	1	0	3	0	0	3	8	0	123	10	9	12	17	3	653	8	1

98

DETAILED STATEMENT OF THE ANNUAL EXPENDITURE ON ACCOUNT OF THE SEVERAL PARKS AND GARDENS, FOR THE YEAR ENDING MARCH 31, 1891.

NAME OF PARK.	Salaries and Wages.	Rates and Taxes.	Tithe Rents.	Garden Tools and Appliances.	Seeds, Plants, and Shrubs.	Payments for Services of Police Band.	Gravel and Asphalting.	Building, Repairs, Painting, &c.	Gas, Coal, Coke, Stationery, Uniforms, and General Maintenance	Total Amount of Expenditure 1891.
	£ s. d.	£ s. d.	£ s. d.	£ s. d.	£ s. d.	£ s. d.	£ s. d.	£ s. d.	£ s. d.	£ s. d.
Aston Park	429 0 6	76 0 10	0 8 0	14 14 7	20 17 6	18 0 0	18 5 6	88 18 4	76 2 1	723 19 0
Cannon Hill Park	*663 4 4	58 15 10	6 11	34 7 0	11 4 0	18 0 0	85 10 0	122 2 5	114 8 0	*1107 18 6
Victoria Park	499 18 0	21 17 0	5 4	13 14 6	9 12 5	18 0 0	10 0 0	103 10 0	62 14 6	747 11 6
Caldthorpe Park	185 12 8	24 7 11	4 11 6	10 13 0	9 4 11		5 0 0	61 8 2	28 6 5	347 4 7
Adderley Park	72 18 0	14 5 1		5 6 3	0 6 0		4 19 0	8 7 4	14 8 2	120 10 4
Burbury Street Recreation Ground	63 5 4	13 5 0		5 8 0	1 17 0	18 0 0	166 19 3	6 14 8	10 3 11	285 13 2
Highgate Park	212 2 0	7 7 3	3 0 4	9 15 3	0 19 0	18 0 0	15 0 0	5 0 6	21 1 9	292 6 1
Summerfield Park	251 15 0	31 12 10	5 12 9	11 9 9	5 4 0	18 0 0	23 11 3	66 13 8	26 12 4	439 19 4
Park Street	150 8 0			1 13 8	2 6 0		26 7 5	96 13 8	10 4 11	287 14 5
St. Mary's	68 14 0			7 5 6	4 11 0		78 7 7	6 6 2	2 11 8	167 17 1
Street Enclosures	57 4 0				4 0 17 9		9 7 7	21 10 6	0 14 4	89 14 8
Whitacre Plantation	23 0 9								14 19 3	37 19 3
Trees in Streets	54 12 2				3 18 8				2 11 11	60 19 9
Rednal Hills	54 12 0	2 6 6						1 0 0	8 15 0	66 13 6
Superintendent's Salary	182 0 0									182 0 0
Totals	2968 3 3	8249 18 3	21 16 10	114 7 2	70 18 3	108 0 0	443 8 2	587 14 1	393 14 9	4958 1 2

*This amount is exclusive of Superintendent's Salary.

SUMMARY OF DETAILS RELATING TO THE SEVERAL PARKS AND GARDENS.

Name of Parks and Gardens.	Districts in which the Parks and Gardens are situated.	Cost to the Corporation, including the whole or part of Purchase, Laying out, Fencing in, &c.	Gifts to the Corporation by various Donors.	Name of Donors.	By whom Opened.
Aston Park	Parish of Aston (N.E.)	£26,750	*£24,000	*Shareholders in the original Aston Park Co. and by various Donors	{ Her Majesty the Queen { Sir John Ratcliff, Mayor † Mr. W. Holliday, Mayor
Cannon Hill Park	Parish of Kings Norton (S.W.)	...	57 acres of Land, Laying out, Fencing in, and Buildings complete	Miss Ryland	Mr. Ald. Biggs, Mayor
Victoria Park	Bordesley Ward (S.E.)	£10,000	About 40 acres of Land, and £6,000 towards Laying out and subsequent improvements	Miss Ryland	Mr. Ald. Jesse Collings, Mayor
Calthorpe Park	Edgbaston Ward (S.)	£1,350	31 acres of Land	Lord Calthorpe and family	H.R.H. the Duke of Cambridge
Adderley Park	Duddeston Ward (E.)	...	About 10 acres of Land for 999 years, at a peppercorn rent of 5s. per annum	Mr. Chas. Bowyer Adderley	Mr. Thomas R. Hodgson, Mayor
Burbury Street Recreation Ground	All Saints' (N.)	£14,522	About 4 acres of Land, Laying out, Fencing in, and Park-keeper's Lodge, &c.	Mr. William Middlemore	Mr. Ald. William Kenrick, Mayor
Highgate Park	Deritend (S.E.)	£14,838	About 1 acre of Land for construction of New Entrance	Mr. Weiss	Mr. Ald. Joseph Chamberlain, Mayor
Summerfield Park	Rotton Park Ward (N.W.)	£7,132	...	...	Mr. Ald. George Baker, Mayor
Park, St. Gardens	St. Bartholomew's Ward (Central)	...	About 4½ acres on Lease for a term of 21 years, at a nominal Rent	...	Mr. Ald. R. Chamberlain, Mayor
St. Mary's Gardens	St. Mary's Ward (Central)	£1,500	About 30 acres	Mr. W. C. A. Smith-Ryland	Mr. Ald. Thomas Avery, Mayor
Balsall Heath Recreation Ground	Balsall Heath Ward	£3,500	From 30 to 40 acres on Lease for a term of 21 years from Dec. 5th, 1869, at a nominal Rent of £5 per annum, paid by Lord Windsor	...	...
Walmer Recreation Ground	St. Stephen's Ward (N.)	...	...	...	...
Rednal and Bilberry Hills	Rednal, near Bromsgrove, Worcestershire	{ On Lease for a Term of 99 years, from Mar. 25, 1891, at a Ground Rent of £239 11s. 8d. per annum }	...	{ By various Donors and by Public Subscription } Lord Windsor	Sir Thomas Martineau, Mayor

* Shares to the value of £9,000 were surrendered by the shareholders of the original Aston Park Company, and the Buildings, with other Improvements carried out by them, at an estimated cost of £8,000. Donations were also given towards the purchase of the Park by the Corporation, viz.—by Messrs. G. and A. Dixon, £2,000; Miss Ryland, £1,000; Mr. Thomas Lloyd, £1,030; Mr. G. F. Muntz, £1,000; and £2,000 by other Donors.

† Opened free to the Public on the 22nd of September, 1864, by W. Holliday, Esq., Mayor.

101
SUMMARY OF DETAILS RELATING TO THE SEVERAL PARKS AND GARDENS (continued).

Name of Parks and Gardens.	Date of Public Opening.	Total area of each Park.			Approx. area Apportioned to Ornamental Gardens, Walks, &c.			Approx. area of Land set apart for Games and General Recreation.			Area of Boating Pools in each Park.	Area of Asphalte or Limestone Paving for Playgrounds.	Area of Greenhouses.	Number of Men employed at each Park.	Income from all sources during the year ending March 31, 1891			Working Expenditure during the year ending March 31, 1891.		
		a.	r.	p.	a.	r.	p.	a.	r.	p.					£	s.	d.	£	s.	d.
Aston Park	June 15, 1858 †Sept. 22, 1864	49	3	18	15	0	34	3	3	18	...	...	2817 sq. ft.	8	68	4	9	723	19	0
Cannon Hill Park	Sept. 1, 1873	57	0	13	35	0	22	0	0	13	One, 15000 sq. yds. One, 10200 sq. yds.	979 sq. yds.	3918 sq. ft.	10	329	12	0	*1289	18	6
Victoria Park	April 5, 1879	43	2	22	27	0	16	2	2	22	One, 15000 sq. yds.	...	1062 sq. ft.	9	174	7	0	747	11	7
Calthorpe Park	June 1, 1857	31	1	13	5	0	26	1	1	13	...	...	...	2	55	9	0	347	4	4
Adderley Park	Aug. 30, 1856	10	0	22	2	0	8	0	0	22	...	...	...	1	11	16	0	120	10	2
Burbury Street Recreation Ground	Dec. 1, 1877	4	1	3	...	...	...	4	1	3	...	8710 sq. yds.	...	1	...	...	...	285	13	1
Highgate Park	June 2, 1876	8	3	28	7	3	8	1	0	20	...	5445 sq. yds.	...	4	1	6	6	292	6	4
Summerfield Park	July 29, 1876	34	1	29	10	0	24	1	1	29	...	5047 sq. yds.	...	4	11	1	4	439	19	5
Park St. Gardens	June 25, 1880	4	1	35	2	0	...	...	...	...	...	5970 sq. yds.	360 sq. ft.	3	...	...	...	287	14	1
Street Enclosures	...	2	3	24	...	...	...	...	...	...	...	...	...	1	...	...	...	167	17	8
St. Mary's Gardens	Oct. 16, 1882	...	...	...	...	...	...	...	...	...	...	...	...	1	...	...	...	89	14	3
Whitacre Plantation	...	...	...	...	...	...	...	...	...	...	...	...	...	...	...	...	...	37	19	9
Trees in Streets	...	...	...	...	...	...	...	...	...	...	...	...	...	...	...	...	...	60	19	...
Balsall Heath Recreation Ground	...	4	1	20	...	...	...	...	...	...	...	...	...	...	...	...	...	...	...	...
Walmer Recreation Ground	...	2	1	29	...	...	...	...	...	...	...	...	...	...	...	...	...	...	...	...
Rednal and Bilberry Hills	May 19, 1888	82	2	21	...	...	...	...	...	...	...	10000 sq. yds.	...	1	1	11	6	66	13	6
Nechells Recreation Ground	...	9	1	9	...	...	...	...	...	...	...	...	...	...	...	...	...	...	...	...

† Free on its acquisition by the Corporation.   * This amount includes the Superintendent's Salary.

102
SUMMARY OF DETAILS RELATING TO THE SEVERAL PARKS AND GARDENS (continued.)

Name of Parks and Gardens.	Amount of Loans Repaid during the year ending March 31, 1891.	Amount of Interest Repaid during the year ending March 31, 1891.	Amount of Loans Borrowed up to March 31, 1891.	Period during which the Loans are Repayable.	Amount of Loans Repaid up to March 31, 1891.	Value of Fire Insurance Policies on Buildings, and amount of Premiums. Amount.	Premium.
	£ s. d.	£ s. d.	£ s. d.		£ s. d.	£ s. d.	£ s. d.
Aston Park ...	311 11 2	558 14 6	26750 0 0	50 years at 3½ and 3 %	12188 8 4	350 0 0	0 9 9
Cannon Hill Park	...	...	...	...	...	2380 0 0	2 16 0
Victoria Park ...	240 17 0	316 9 11	10000 0 0	30 years at 3½ and 3 %	1818 8 8	1300 0 0	1 7 3
Calthorpe Park	45 0 0	25 10 10	1350 0 0	30 years at 3½ and 3 %	742 10 0	400 0 0	0 8 6
Adderley Park	...	...	...	...	...	...	...
Burbury Street Recreation Ground	...	...	...	...	...	...	...
Highgate Park	422 17 0	503 16 4	14522 0 0	30 years at 3½ and 4 %	4522 18 10	300 0 0	0 4 6
Summerfield Park	91 7 10	420 17 9	14838 0 0	60 and 30 years at 3½, 3, and 2¾ %	868 11 9	300 0 0	0 4 9
Park Street Gardens	40 10 0	252 19 1	7132 0 0	60 years at 3½ %	312 14 2	1000 0 0	0 15 0
St. Mary's Gardens	45 8 8	47 17 0	1500 0 0	25 years at 3½ %	283 5 5	...	...
Street Enclosures	...	...	...	...	...	...	...
Trees in Streets	...	...	...	...	...	...	...
Walmer Recreation Ground ...	...	...	...	...	...	...	...
Rednal and Bilberry Hill	...	...	...	...	...	...	...

www.ingramcontent.com/pod-product-compliance
Lightning Source LLC
Chambersburg PA
CBHW030311170426
43202CB00009B/956